Legend and Lore of the Guadalupe Mountains

Legend and Lore
of the Guadalupe Mountains

Mountains

W. C. Jameson

University of New Mexico Press   Albuquerque

Library of Congress Cataloging-in-Publication Data

Jameson, W. C., 1942–

  Legend and lore of the Guadalupe Mountains / W.C. Jameson.

    p. cm.

  Includes bibliographical references and index.

  ISBN-13: 978-0-8263-4217-1 (pbk. : alk. paper)

  1. Guadalupe Mountains (N.M. and Tex.)—History—Anecdotes.

  2. Guadalupe Mountains (N.M. and Tex.)—History, Local—Anecdotes.

  3. Guadalupe Mountains (N.M. and Tex.)—Biography—Anecdotes.

  4. Legends—Guadalupe Mountains (N.M. and Tex.)

  5. Folklore—Guadalupe Mountains (N.M. and Tex.)

  I. Title.

  F392.G86J358 2007

  976.4'94—dc22

                        2006031822

Design and composition: Melissa Tandysh

For Jack and Jo Kincaid, Nickel Creek friends
who know the mountain and the people
better than most, and whose
home and café provided
incomparable refuge,
meals, conversation,
and camaraderie
over the years.

Contents

Preface

As soon as I was old enough to cadge rides to the Guadalupe Mountains from my boyhood home in Ysleta, Texas, I spent most of my spare time in that fascinating place. The 110-mile distance seemed a long way for a fourteen-year-old in the 1950s, but over the years I came to love the trip, for it filled me with anticipation as I approached the range.

Not only had I traveled far on my first visit to the Guadalupes, I also felt as though I had been transported back to a time and place of Apache Indians, outlaws, and treasure hunters. I had long heard tales of ghosts and spirits which many believed dwelt in the range, and on that first day, alone in a deep, quiet canyon, I felt their presence like the desert feels rain.

Like many others, I was first introduced to the Guadalupe Mountains through the writings of the esteemed Texas folklorist and author J. Frank Dobie. Dobie, who collected and wrote about tales of hauntings and lost mines and buried treasures, had a special empathy for the region like no other. As a fifth-grader, I remember exploring the pages of *Coronado's Children* and growing fascinated at the descriptions of this remote territory, of the fortunes found and lost among the rocks, canyons, and peaks of the Guadalupes. Dobie's stories of prospectors and treasure hunters stirred within my young breast a heretofore unknown fever and yearning for exploration, a latent and essential need for the search, the quest. Utterly captivated, I read and reread *Coronado's Children*, memorizing the details relative to lost gold, to the deep canyons, to this remote homeland of the Mescalero Apache.

Even at that juvenescent and unfocused age of eleven, I found myself longing to travel to the Guadalupe Mountains, to walk in the canyons, to climb the peaks, to drink the waters from the springs that broke from the flanks of the escarpment.

During the next few years, I searched for and read everything I could find by Dobie, and to this day his work holds a special place in my personal library, books that I return to from time to time to relive the excitement of that distinct time of my youth.

As the years rolled by I moved on to other things—I wrote books of my own and held a number of different jobs ranging from unloading boxcars to teaching at a university. Few of those activities, however, provided the same excitement I derived from my initial encounter with the Guadalupe Mountains.

The first time I traveled to the Guadalupes, I was quite unprepared for what I encountered. Riding east with a neighbor who had some cattle business to conduct in the area, I left my home one morning at five. We were still some forty miles from the range when the rising sun profiled the mountains. I was thrilled by the sight, for looming thousands of feet from the desert floor were the silhouettes of El Capitan and Guadalupe Peaks, vertical geologic masterpieces that alternately invited and threatened. To the north and west of them, the seemingly razor edge of the western escarpment stretched into the distance like a massive and extensive fortress wall. As we crossed the salt flats which lie just to the west of the range, we could see a mist settling among the higher elevations which lent an aura of mystery and remoteness to the environment.

After being dropped off near the Pinery, the tumbled-down remains of a more-than-century-old Butterfield Stage station at the mouth of Pine Spring Canyon, I fitted a canteen to my belt, filled my lungs with crisp, clean mountain air, and began my adventure. After twenty minutes of hiking along a stock trail, I found myself within the realm of a huge gorge, steep walls of exposed limestone rising on each side. At that point, I knew I had been captured by the spirit and magic of this incredible range for all time.

On that long ago day I explored several small caves I found, walked up deep arroyos, and sat peacefully in the shade of a glorious Texas madrone as I marveled at the stunning rock formations in the deeper reaches of the canyon. I followed game trails and stock trails, and when I ran out of trails I set out across the rocky canyon floor, weaving my way among prickly pear and cholla, among boulders and rattlesnakes, thrilling at small discoveries with each step.

I originally came to the Guadalupes believing, hoping I could find some of the lost treasures of which Dobie wrote. I searched for them long and hard, but once in the embrace of Pine Spring Canyon, I realized there was so much more to the place than just gold. Even as an unsophisticated youth, I felt a special connection here, a strong one, an important one that was to stay with me for the rest of my life. I experienced a rudimentary kinship with the Mescalero Apache who once lived, hunted, and fought in this range; to the Spanish explorers who many believe came to the Guadalupe

Mountains in search of gold; to the early settlers; to the prospectors. I felt as part of the rock, the ages-old, weathered limestone that dominated those mountains. In the years to come, the feeling was to grow stronger, and I knew that I would return again and again.

When I was finally picked up for the ride home, the sun was only moments away from setting and Pine Spring Canyon was blanketed with shadows. Though I had hiked all day and had eaten nothing save for a dry biscuit I brought with me, I was neither hungry nor tired. Instead, I was exhilarated from my experience, from my explorations. I wanted to stay, but was expected at home. I knew I would return at the first opportunity.

During the next decade, I came to the Guadalupe Mountains as often as possible—weekends, holidays, and summers. With a single canteen of water and a cloth sack filled with jerky and corn tortillas, I spent uncountable days and nights camping in the high country and in the canyons. Sometimes I remained as long as four or five days at a time, running out of water and slaking my thirst by licking early morning dew from the leaves, and finally coming out tired, hungry, and thirsty, but always enriched beyond measure by the experience.

In the mountains I encountered a variety of wildlife—deer, elk, eagles, peregrine falcons, horned toads, and wild turkeys. In the soft earth of the canyon floors near streams I found the tracks of bear. My camps were open and primitive, and many a night I simply reclined against the bole of a thick pine and listened to the hooting of the owls in the trees above and the gobbling of turkeys in the canyons below. Once, I heard the scream of a panther.

Here, I also discovered the delights and rewards of solitude. Rarely did I encounter humans; the few I came in contact with in those days were either ranch hands or forest service employees.

During my extended periods of solitude, I discovered special connections to the land, connections that convinced me I was more kindred to the stone and tree, to the deer and panther, than I was to the so-called civilization I'd left to come here.

Finding lost treasure in the form of precious metals became less and less of a passion for me. I was learning the differences between lore and fact, and I cultivated an appreciation for both. At first, I expected to find treasure, but as time passed and other passions came to the fore, I cared little about riches. By this time, the mountains themselves became the treasure I needed.

Nonetheless, I found gold. Once, while exploring a small, narrow, twisting cave, I discovered a small cache of gold nuggets. The leather sacks in which the nuggets had once been placed had long since been nibbled away by rodents, leaving only remnants, and the small piles of gold, covered in a layer of fine dust, lay close together upon the floor of the cave. Nearby were an abandoned ax head and a small mattock. I placed some of the gold in a pocket and left the cave.

During the time I had roamed and explored the range, the Guadalupe Mountains grew more precious to me than gold, more cherished than any piece of geography I could name. The Guadalupes became a treasure of peace and serenity.

I also found treasure in the form of people. During my visits to the mountains I came to know many of the residents of the area—ranchers, herders, cowhands, café operators, park rangers, and others. Most of them evinced a strong attachment to the range comparable to my own. Even though they barely eked out a living, none wished to leave. When they regarded the mountains, it was with a special reverence for place I'd never encountered anywhere else.

As time went by and as I visited the range more frequently, I stopped regularly at the local cafés and taverns. Gradually, I came to know the folk who lived here. At first I quietly sipped coffee at a table and listened to the regulars talk. At the Pine Springs Café, I would eavesdrop for hours on a cluster of long-time Guadalupe Mountains residents speaking of the history of the area, of old-timers who had lived in the area for decades, of exploring remote reaches of the range. From them I discovered another kind of treasure—the stories, tales, and legends associated with the land.

Sometimes the Guadalupians talked about the tales of buried treasure long associated with these mountains. Other times they spoke of ghosts and spirits that many believed resided in the dark interior of the range. Often, they shared personal experiences and exchanged stories of strange things encountered high in the mountains and far from the eyes of travelers and visitors, tales of unexplainable happenings, stories filled with mystery and wonder. The regulars seldom shared their stories with outsiders, and when a newcomer entered, the conversations shifted to other topics.

In time, I was included, even welcomed, and from those strong and durable western mountain folk I learned much more about that precious piece of geography, and the people, places, and things associated with it. What continued to thrill me the most, however, were the stories, the tales that had their roots in the range, tales that grew out of the region like the century plant and the madrone.

For hours I sat inside the tiny café and listened to the reminiscences of Walter and Bertha Glover, two long-time residents who had carved out a living decades earlier raising cattle and goats. Occasional Pine Springs residents were Pauline and Ben Wattson. Ben, called Tio Ben by the locals, had a hook for one hand and claimed to be over one hundred years old. Members of the Hughes ranching family in Dog Canyon had lived in the range for over a century and had seen many changes. National Park Service Ranger Roger Reisch, ranch foreman Noel Kincaid, café operators Jack and Jo Kincaid, and Dell City sheep rancher and tavern owner Bonnie Prather all provided pieces of history and lore of the Guadalupe Mountains. It was from such people as these that I learned the bones of many of the tales presented in this book.

Today I continue to visit the Guadalupe Mountains and the people, and both remain a source of stories and inspiration. After four decades, I continue to learn from them. Sadly, some of the people are gone, and I think about them often. The sensations and connections I initially experienced during my first visits to the mountains remain, however, and I suspect they always will.

In 1966, the National Park Service formally acquired the Guadalupe Mountains and worked hard to make the high country more accessible to visitors. I resented this new intrusion into what I considered my mountains, but gradually became accustomed to the presence of park employees.

Since the Guadalupe Mountains have become a national park, hundreds of articles and features pertaining to the range have appeared in magazines devoted to travelers, tourists, backpackers, photographers, and naturalists. Scholars around the country come to the range to study biological and geological phenomena. These days, one is more likely to encounter a biologist in the mountains than a rattlesnake.

Even though the Guadalupe Mountains now receive more visitors than ever, they have somehow maintained a sense of remoteness, of mystery, of intangible connection to the past and to the spirits of those who once roamed here.

There are many tales associated with the Guadalupe Mountains. Many of them are factual, having been historically documented. Others are part of the legend and lore. A few are bizarre.

Some, by no means all, are presented here, a variety ranging from the authenticated to the conjectural. Like the people who live here, each is different. Some are plain and straightforward, others stretch one's ability to believe, but not the desire.

Like the people who told me the tales, they are all products of the mountains.

Acknowledgments

I owe a large debt to many people, living and gone, who shared their stories, adventures, knowledge, and time with me over the past decades: Walter and Bertha Glover, Tio Ben and Pauline Wattson, Noel Kincaid, Jack Kincaid, Roger Reisch, Bonnie Prather, members of the Dog Canyon Hughes family, and dozens of Guadalupe Mountains National Park Service employees.

Special thanks to Laurie Wagner Buyer who allowed me to introduce her to the wonders of this magnificent landscape, who accompanied me on several trips into the heart of the range, and who applied her incomparable editorial expertise to the final draft of this manuscript.

Introduction

THE GUADALUPE MOUNTAINS are the highest mountain range in the state of Texas, with Guadalupe Peak rising to an altitude of 8,751 feet above sea level. The tallest peaks of the range are in Culberson County, but the range itself, shaped somewhat like a V, straddles the Texas-New Mexico line, extending for miles. In the northeastern section of the V can be found Carlsbad Caverns and Lechuguilla Cave, the latter, speleologists tell us, is the largest cavern system in the world. The northwestern trending part of the V grades into the Sacramento Mountains in New Mexico, just north of which lies the Mescalero Apache Indian reservation.

The Guadalupe Mountains, an uplifted barrier reef composed principally of fossilized algae, has been home to Apaches, wolves, bear, mountain lion, large rattlesnakes, and, according to folklore, ghosts and buried treasures. This remote land has been visited and lived in by early Americans called Basketmakers, by Apaches and Comanches, Spanish conquistadores, Mexicans, and more recently white men who have established ranches and farms in the region. These days, most who come to the mountains are tourists, photographers, campers, hikers, and backpackers.

Over the centuries, the Guadalupe Mountains offered many things. For uncountable generations, they provided a living and habitat for primitive man who harvested wild foods, hunted game, drank of and bathed in the spring waters, and who occasionally managed to coax a few meager crops out of the mostly dry lowland soils.

For at least a few hundred years, these mountains were home to the Mescalero Apaches, battle-hardened warriors feared by many

FIG. 1 El Capitan Peak, the southernmost point of the Guadalupe Mountains. (PHOTO COURTESY LAURIE WAGNER BUYER.)

other tribes as well as by early Mexican and Anglo settlers. This high, remote, and easy-to-defend region suited them nicely, and the abundance of mescal, or century plant, provided an important food staple that was eaten boiled, roasted, or dried. Mescal was even fermented to make a strong alcoholic drink. To the Mescalero Apache, the mescal was a fundamental resource for life, much like the bison to the Plains Indians. Remains of their campgrounds can still be found in the high country.

When the Mescaleros were finally driven out of the Guadalupe Mountains, white men intent on farming and ranching moved in, and subsequently the environment provided for large herds of cattle, goats, and sheep, both in the high country and along the foothills and flanks of the range. Though not as extensive as in previous years, ranching is still pursued in this sometimes harsh and forbidding area with varying degrees of success.

Former Texas Folklore Society president J. Frank Dobie is responsible for bringing the Guadalupe Mountains to the attention of the general public. In his wonderful book *Coronado's Children*, Dobie devoted a chapter to several extraordinary tales of lost mines and buried treasures associated with this region. The inherent appeal of hidden wealth, along with Dobie's captivating style of writing, thrilled and enticed many who came to these mountains to find riches. Evidence indicates some actually located treasure here. Over the years, however, most of the visitors to the Guadalupe Mountains—the explorers, the searchers, the ranchers, the hikers, and campers—returned to their homes with a different kind of treasure. They brought back with them a treasury of fascinating tales pertinent to this exciting, oftentimes mysterious, and sometimes dangerous range.

As much as any geographic area in Texas, the Guadalupe Mountains have been a fertile source of extraordinary legend and lore. When a region serves up such a rich fount of stories, folklorists seek reasons why. Outside of Dobie, however, virtually no one has devoted any attention to the tales associated with the range. To those few who have taken the time to examine this setting in detail, some important folktale-producing elements are easily identified: remoteness, mystery, extreme ruggedness, a forbidding landscape, and a multicultural component associated with settlement and visitation.

Remoteness is a key characteristic of the Guadalupe Mountains. Located in the northern reaches of the Chihuahuan Desert, the Guadalupes were, historically, well off the beaten path, not along any commonly traveled route. Even today, lying adjacent to Highway 62–180 which connects El Paso, Texas, to Carlsbad, New Mexico, the Guadalupe Mountains attract relatively few visitors, and area cafés and gas stations often struggle to remain in business. Many do not, and the highway landscape is littered with failed enterprises.

Remoteness, many contend, can be an essential ingredient for mystery, and the Guadalupe Mountains have maintained an aura of mystery for centuries. Because early explorers and travelers in this region knew very little about the range and, save for the Apaches, seldom ventured into the higher elevations, an element of the unknown, even a kind of terror, crept into reports and journals that resulted from such expeditions. Early writers often wondered in print what lay behind the conifer-fringed rim of the limestone escarpment.

The extreme rough, broken, and sometimes dangerous terrain associated with this mountainous landscape must also be considered. Because of the steep, rocky trails, the parched desert environment surrounding the range, the scarceness of water in the high country, and the presence of Apaches as well as bear, mountain

FIG. 2 Mescal plant in bloom.
(PHOTO COURTESY LAURIE WAGNER BUYER.)

lion, wolves, and other creatures, early visitors were often discouraged from venturing too far into the mountains, particularly the deep wilderness of the interior.

Historically, travel into and through the Guadalupe Mountains was difficult for anything but horses and mules, and even for them it wasn't particularly easy. Wagons filled with west-bound settlers struggled with the route through Guadalupe Pass, but this trail was generally avoided. After eleven months of maintaining a station in Guadalupe Pass, the Butterfield Overland Mail abandoned the route for a more southerly and less difficult one.

Though they eventually prevailed as a result of superior numbers and firepower, U.S. Army cavalry units experienced great difficulty traveling the rough slopes and ridges in pursuit of cattle- and horse-stealing Mescalero Apaches.

The multicultural aspect of the Guadalupe Mountains no doubt added to the mix of elements that spawned numerous and lively tales from the region. Though never proven, evidence suggests that early Spanish explorers visited the range to search for precious minerals. Some claim they may have established a brief residence here, living peacefully with the natives; others contend they conducted warfare with the residents and were killed off.

Mexican traders regularly crossed the range through the pass during the 1800s. Though Mexican settlement in the area was never great, it is likely they camped here and availed themselves of the game and waters once so abundant along the slopes. Undoubtedly, Mexicans and Mescaleros had contact with one another during that time.

Outlaws, prospectors, and recluses came to these mountains. Some stayed for a time, but eventually all departed, or died.

Anglo ranchers gained a strong foothold in the region around the beginning of the twentieth century and, with varying degrees of success, carved out a living raising livestock.

The interior high country of the Guadalupes is visited more frequently these days than in the past—hikers and backpackers are lured into the picturesque setting by word-of-mouth or attractive photographs and articles found in travel and outdoor magazines. With visitation generally small by National Park Service standards, packers who take the time and effort to climb the steep, rocky trails and spend a few days in the higher elevations share the environment with deer, elk, bear, snakes, and myriad other wildlife. Despite so-called improvements inflicted onto the Guadalupe Mountains National Park by the NPS, there remain significant elements of mystery, solitude, and challenging landscape.

Once in a great while, a hiker or camper will come out of the range with another story, another strange experience or sighting, or another interesting discovery. A rancher may relate an odd encounter or a strange event to one of his neighbors. These stories and accounts are told and retold, and eventually add to the growing trove of legend and lore spawned by the incredible and exciting land of the Guadalupe Mountains.

Chapter One

The Legacy of the Spaniards

IN MARCH 1536, a scouting party consisting of five armored, lance-bearing Spaniards had been sent to investigate a section of the rugged coastline along the Gulf of California near the present-day city of Guaymas, Mexico. Their assignment was to reconnoiter the region and report back within a week to their commanding officer who remained with the main company of conquistadores encamped several miles inland. Rounding a rocky bend along the irregular shore during the second day of their mission, the scouts came upon a naked man crawling on his hands and knees and muttering incoherencies. The man, deeply tanned and gaunt, was a Spaniard, and he was accompanied by a black man and two Indians, all in similar condition. This strange party had been without sufficient food for several days and the members were clearly starving. Perceiving their wretched condition, the scouts offered the group what little fresh water and food they carried. The next morning when the white man was finally able to speak, he related an amazing story.

His name was Cabeza de Vaca. Eight years earlier, he claimed, he was in command of a ship that was part of the Pánfilo de Narváez expedition, for whom he was treasurer. The ship wrecked on the Florida shore and the company, which consisted of three hundred men, journeyed inland. Needing food and fresh water in this unknown land, the sailors split up into several small groups and entered the forest in search of game. Captain de Vaca and his black servant, Estevanico, along with a dozen crewmen, were following a well-used game trail through the dense forest when they were attacked by Indians. Outnumbered, the Spaniards fled into the woods, becoming lost. For weeks they wandered directionless, unable to relocate the coastline or their companions. Continued attacks forced them deeper into the forest. Sometimes they were able to find game, other times they went days without sustenance. Hostile encounters with the natives were frequent and the Spaniards soon learned to avoid Indian settlements.

For weeks the Spaniards fled westward, crossing treacherous swamps and passing through dark forests. Weeks of wandering turned into months, months into years, and the wooded country through which they traveled gradually opened up into plains and then desert. On rare occasions, the Spaniards encountered friendly Indians who offered food. Sometimes the natives would accompany the travelers for several days at a time.

The quest for survival continued for eight long years, and during that time de Vaca and his followers continued west, ever hoping for succor. Along the way, all but the captain and Estevanico perished.

While trekking through the arid lands of what is now New Mexico, the two men were overtaken by an Indian hunting party. It was apparent to the Indians that the strangers had covered a great distance on few provisions, so they were invited to their camp to share the fruits of a recent bison kill. Here, de Vaca and Estevanico were fed and provided shelter, and the two men fascinated their hosts with descriptions of lands far to the east from which they had come, descriptions the Spaniards rendered in crude sign language.

During the weeks de Vaca and Estevanico remained with the Indians, they could not help but notice most of them wore arm and ankle bands, jewelry, and a variety of other ornaments fashioned from gold and precious stones. When the Spaniards asked about the items, they were told by the chief that farther north there existed seven great cities filled with such treasures that were dug from the rock of the nearby mountains. Sometimes, said the chief, the residents of those cities would journey southward and trade some of their gold and jewels for salt and hides. The kingdom of seven cities was called Cibola.

Cabeza de Vaca considered traveling to Cibola to witness for himself the great cities described by the chief, but he retained the hope that by continuing westward he would encounter some of his countrymen. Finally, de Vaca and Estevanico, now well-fed and rested, proceeded on their journey, this time accompanied by eleven members of the tribe.

The Spanish scouts listened in awe to the story told by de Vaca, and felt a keen admiration for this countryman and his companion who survived such an incredible ordeal. After two days of ministering to the travelers, the scouts escorted de Vaca and his party to the main body of conquistadores. Here, in the presence of the officers, the tale of escape and survival across much of the continent was retold many times.

Having earlier observed first hand the fabulous treasures of the

Peruvian Inca, several of the Spanish officers were intrigued at the possibilities of finding cities filled with gold and other riches in the north. Weeks later, de Vaca, Estevanico and the others were delivered to the local governor where, once again, the account of the incredible journey was related.

The story of the seven golden cities of Cibola eventually made its way up the Spanish chain of command, and months later reached Viceroy Antonio de Mendoza. The viceroy pondered the possibilities of exploring the region to the north in the hope of locating the golden cities, and finally in 1540 named Francisco Vasquez de Coronado, recently named governor of the Nueva Galicia Province, to lead an exploration party to locate the seven cities of Cibola.

The young Coronado was given command of soldiers, miners, engineers, and Indian slaves to search for the fabled cities and return with great wealth. The party consisted of 300 Spaniards, over 1,000 Indians, 1,000 horses, and herds of sheep and pigs to serve as a food supply. With Estevanico to lead the way back to the deserts of the north, Coronado felt confident he would find the seven cities and their associated treasures, which he would personally deliver to the viceroy. Coronado felt certain his military and political careers would be enhanced as a result of his anticipated success.

For two years Coronado searched for the seven cities of gold, and the journey across the deserts and plains of the north was often fraught with hardship and disaster. Along the way he suffered losses of livestock and men to raiders, disease, starvation, and thirst. Many deserted. His quest took him through the panhandle of Texas and as far north and east as the plains of Kansas, but the cities of gold continued to elude him.

While Coronado's army traveled through the *llano estacado*, the staked plains of the Texas panhandle, a group of twenty soldiers separated from the main party. Some who have studied Coronado's journey claim the commander sent them to the southwest into a mysterious mountain range to investigate rumors of a lost tribe and abundant gold. Other scholars are convinced the soldiers simply deserted. Regardless of the reason, a score of mounted conquistadores arrived in the foothills of the Guadalupe Mountains about three weeks later following a difficult crossing of the windy and waterless plains.

So different was this region from the dry, hostile, and forbidding land through which they had traveled so long! Here the soldiers found fresh water springs gurgling from the flanks of the escarpment, the cool environs of pine and spruce forested uplands,

FIG. 3 Rugged landscape of the Guadalupe Mountains
that greeted early Spanish explorers.
(PHOTO COURTESY LAURIE WAGNER BUYER.)

and wild game aplenty. Numerous shelter caves afforded protection, and small bands of friendly Indians shared their food and showed the newcomers how to identify and prepare edible plants for consumption.

No golden cities here, but the Spaniards apparently discovered some gold in rock outcrops at one or more locations in the mountains. While the source of that gold remains a mystery to this day, Indian legends handed down over the generations refer to the race of mounted white men who came and taught the people how to dig the shining metal from the rock and fashion it into ornaments.

Rather than return to Coronado and report the discovery, the Spaniards decided to remain in the pleasant mountain range. No longer did they wish to march horseback across dusty terrain in long columns and subsist on scanty rations. Never again would they have to take orders and engage in battle with hostile savages. Living in harmony with the Indians in the Guadalupes, perhaps even intermarrying, the Spaniards carved out a comfortable existence as hunters and gatherers. This high country afforded a fine living compared to that of being a soldier, and knowing that Coronado could neither spare the men nor the time to search for them, the twenty deserters settled into their new home.

Years passed, and the gold ore continued to be mined from the rocks of the Guadalupe Mountains. While some was used for ornaments, most of it, after being separated from the quartz matrix, was placed in pouches and baskets and cached in convenient hiding places—caves, rock crevices, mine shafts. Since gold was never important to the Indians, and since it was unnecessary for survival in the mountains, the Spaniards eventually ceased mining altogether. According to the legend, the mines were closed down and covered over.

With the passage of generations, descendants of the Indians and Spaniards still living in the area occasionally retrieved some of the cached gold to make ornaments, but in time the hiding places were forgotten.

Years later, gradual changes in climate led to an extended period of severe drought throughout the region. Deprived of needed moisture, the forest grew sere and hundreds of trees died. The springs, once so abundant, dried up save for a few. Wild game became scarce. The inhabitants of the Guadalupe Mountains and the surrounding region were forced to move away, taking only what they could carry on their backs. It is doubtful any remembered where the gold was hidden, but if they did it was unlikely they would have been willing to carry away any of the heavy ore. When they left, the gold remained where it was cached years earlier.

The ultimate destination of these early Guadalupe Mountains residents has never been determined and has remained a mystery since scholars first undertook the study of the exodus. What is known for certain is that they never came back.

Some contend the Spanish conquistadores never entered the Guadalupe Mountains at all, and that stories of their presence here are mere whimsy. Others maintain that gold does not and cannot exist in these mountains, that the predominantly limestone strata is not conducive to its formation.

In fact, evidence does exist of the presence of the Spanish in the Guadalupe Mountains. Furthermore, evidence that specific geologic conditions leading to the formation of gold exist beneath the sedimentary rock that makes up most of this range.

In 1959, eighteen-year-old Richard Watts unearthed an oddly shaped piece of metal from several inches of loose dirt, blowsand, and animal debris near the rear wall of a shelter cave in the Guadalupe Mountains. The object was man-made and ancient, but Watts could only guess at the identity and significance. With the help of several scholars associated with the University of Texas, the piece of metal was identified as a breastplate, a piece of Spanish armor similar to the kind worn during the time of Coronado.

During the 1960s, while digging near a former spring close to the white sand dunes just west of the Guadalupe Mountains, a man hunting Indian campsites and artifacts uncovered several animal bones. He guessed rightly that they were from a horse, and lying among the remains were a spur and a small metal buckle. Subsequent examination revealed the items to be of medieval Spanish origin.

In 1971, a hiker found a corroded piece of metal on the ground near the wall of a shallow canyon deep in the range. After cleaning the thick coating of rust from the item, the finder beheld a well-used pick similar to the kind employed by miners. A second cleaning revealed an inscription on the tool which indicated it was forged in Toledo, Spain, in 1526.

As for the oft-disputed existence of gold in the Guadalupe Mountains, many contend, and rightly so, that underground volcanic activity is necessary for its formation. They also contend that no such process ever existed here. They are in error. Within only a few miles of the Guadalupe Mountains, an abundance of exposed igneous intrusive rock exists, ample proof that such activity did indeed occur here. It is completely within the realm of possibility that in the geologic past, molten material from deep below the surface of the earth surged into pockets of faulted and weakened portions of the crust just below this covering of limestone. In 1987, a geographic expedition into the range discovered tiny pieces of igneous intrusive rock along the southeast-facing slope.

Taken together, the accumulating evidence increasingly points to the notion that early Spaniards did visit the Guadalupe Mountains, and that with the possible help of their new Indian friends, mined gold.

Gold was not all that was left behind when the descendants of the conquistadores departed the range. They left an incredible legacy of lore and mystery that characterizes much of this amazing range, a legacy that has given rise to numerous legends and tales that continue to enthrall, entertain, and baffle people today.

Chapter Two

Apache Ghosts

YEARS AFTER THE earliest inhabitants of the Guadalupe Mountains departed, never to return, the range was visited by another tribe, the Mescalero Apaches. The Apaches, once a people who followed the great herds of buffalo throughout the southern Great Plains, were driven from their lands by the powerful Comanche. Successive retreats from their aggressive attackers resulted in the plains Apaches finding refuge in the Guadalupe Mountains.

By the time the Apaches arrived in the Guadalupes, the climate had changed once again. Rains were more frequent, the springs were flowing cool and full, the high altitude forest flourished, and the wild game had returned.

From the desert floor up across the rocky slopes to the highest ridges grew the versatile mescal, a dry land plant that was edible, rich in carbohydrates, and capable of being prepared in a number of ways. The head of the mescal could be roasted, boiled, dried, and stored for long periods. The stems, well over twelve feet tall at maturity and as thick as a man's arm, yielded a pulpy interior rich in nutrients. The blossoms were tasty, and during times of blooming smelled like burnt coconut. The sap, which surged into the stalk during the growing season, could be fermented into a potent liquor.

Furthermore, the fibers from the dried leaves of the mescal plant (also called maguey and century plant) could be twisted into strong cords and ropes and woven into baskets and mats. The long, sharp point at the end of each mescal leaf found use as a sewing needle.

The abundant mescal became the essential food for the tribe as well as for their horses. So important was this food to these mountain dwellers that they became known as the Mescalero Apaches.

When the Mescaleros came to the Guadalupes is not known for certain, but it has been established they were there by the mid-1700s. Raiding parties would occasionally leave the mountain stronghold, travel into Mexico or points west, and return with captured horses, cattle, women, and slaves. Depredations on travelers were frequent, and tales of torture and killing were common. Following each raid, the Mescaleros would escape into the interior highlands of the Guadalupe Mountains.

For over a century, the Mescalero Apaches ruled supreme throughout the Guadalupes and regarded it as their homeland. The mountains served as a natural, near-impregnable fortress few pursuers dared to enter.

As Mescalero raids became more frequent, and as more and more ranchers began losing livestock to the Indians, the United States Army was finally summoned to action. During the winter of 1869, Lt. Howard B. Cushing, along with a force of sixty-five cavalrymen and civilians, entered the Guadalupes from the north and tracked the Mescaleros to their campground high in the mountains. Following a pitched battle, dozens of Apaches were killed and the rest routed, fleeing to the plains below. Though a few stragglers remained in the range for a time, the dominance of the Mescaleros in the Guadalupes had come to an end. Area settlers and ranchers rejoiced at the news that the Apaches were gone.

Or were they? Though the Indians had been chased from the Guadalupe environs, their ghosts, according to many, remained.

As increasing numbers of white settlers moved into the region, talk of Apaches still living in the mountain range was common. Though the Indians were rarely spotted, reports abounded that they could be heard, generally at night. When pressed for details, the settlers claimed that at certain times of the year from somewhere near the bottom of the slope of the prominent south-facing El Capitan Peak, the sounds of drums, chanting, and dancing could be heard. Some even reported spotting the flicker of campfires in this area, but when a few brave men would ride into the canyon to investigate, all sound stopped and nothing could be seen. Eerily, the chanting and drumming started up again once the riders departed.

Today, well over a century later, the sounds of drumming, singing, and dancing are still heard in the area. Hikers returning from Guadalupe Peak late in the evening along the winding trail that leads to the Pine Springs campground have reported hearing the sounds of drums and chants drifting up from below.

During the spring, park visitors hiking late in the day along the old dirt road from Shumard Canyon on the western escarpment sometimes comment on strange drumming sounds coming from somewhere along the slope. Late evening travelers on Highway 62–180 have reported seeing campfires and thin plumes of smoke coming from the canyon in the valley below El Capitan Peak. Each time the area was searched for the source of the mysterious sounds and campfires, nothing was ever found.

Before his death in 1963, James Kaywaykla, a Warm Springs Apache, who, along with his grandmother and sister, survived the 1881 Tres Castillos Massacre in Mexico, provided an explanation for these odd occurrences in the Guadalupe Mountains. Removed from his ancestral home by white soldiers when he was nine years old and formally educated at the Carlisle School for Indians in Pennsylvania, Kaywaykla dictated his recollections of earlier years to noted writer and historian Eve Ball. The aged Kaywaykla told Ball that the strange sounds rising from near the base of the sacred peak came from the ghosts of his ancestors and were related to a traditional Mescalero ceremony. The ghosts, he said, resided in a cave located just above the canyon floor.

At a certain time of the year, according to Kaywaykla, the young Apache women eligible for marriage were, and still are, formally presented in a very old and sacred rite. During the ceremony, the young girl must be dressed in certain Indian finery, all made and decorated by relatives. Covering her upper body was a long, soft, pliable buckskin shirt with fifteen-inch-long fringe. Hundreds of beads and cone-shaped silver bells were sewn onto these garments in a variety of patterns. Knee-length beaded moccasins of soft leather were presented to the girl on the evening prior to the ceremony.

Rounding out the costume were several bracelets, necklaces, earrings, and hairpieces, all made from gold. Once telegraph lines were strung throughout the territory, the Indians found that the copper wire also made beautiful shiny jewelry and they often helped themselves to this convenient source of metal. In recent years, ceremonial jewelry has been manufactured from both metals as well as silver, but old tradition dictated that each ornament was specifically and carefully made for each young girl, hammered and shaped from gold obtained from a secret source which, according to the Apache elders, was located somewhere in the Guadalupe Mountains. Many believe it to be from secret caches of gold originally mined by the Spaniards.

The presentation ceremony described by Kaywaykla started with the Mescalero Apaches during the mid-1700s, but during the ensuing years it has been adopted by members of the Chiricahua and Warm Springs tribes. In order to obtain the gold for the special ornaments, members of these tribes would travel to the Guadalupe Mountains. This range, according to the Mescaleros, is the source of all gold used by the Apaches.

At the opening of each presentation ceremony, the story of its origin is told. In the Guadalupe Mountains, according to the legend, there exists a high mountain resembling a face. Today, this mountain is known as El Capitan Peak, but the Mescaleros called it *Say-a-chee*, and throughout their history it has been regarded as a sacred mountain. Near its base is a mysterious cave, and according to the believers, the spirits that dwell here are called the Earth People and are regarded as the ancestors of the Mescalero Apaches. One of their responsibilities is to keep a perpetual watch for approaching enemies, thus ensuring the safety of the tribe.

Even during the time of Mescalero occupation of the Guadalupe Mountains, the sounds of drumming and singing were often heard coming from somewhere near the base of Say-a-chee, but the unexplainable noises frightened the superstitious Indians and they were afraid to investigate.

One day, a band of Warm Springs Apaches visited the Mescaleros in their Guadalupe stronghold and were told of the sounds coming from near the base of the mountain. One of the visitors was a woman believed to possess great medicine, and she asked to be taken to the site. The Mescaleros tried to dissuade her but she was insistent, and finally several warriors escorted her to the foot of the slope.

Here they found a deep cave with a small opening, and she told her escorts to wait for her while she entered and explored it. The warriors tried to prevent her from going into the mysterious cave, but she ignored them. After she vanished into the darkness, they retreated to a low rise several yards away and prayed for her safe return.

After the medicine woman had been gone for over an hour, the warriors heard faint singing accompanied by the beat of drums, all coming from deep within the cave. Starting out very low at first, the sound gradually increased in volume until it shook the nearby canyon walls. They grew frightened.

The Indian escort waited for a long time and grew concerned that the medicine woman had been killed by the Earth People. Just as they were preparing to return to camp, she called to them from inside the cave. As they peered into the darkness, she emerged, carrying a small white lamb in her arms.

After the medicine woman was escorted back to the camp, she told the others of what transpired in the cave. During her conversation with the Earth People, she said, she was instructed to make preparations for an important ceremony. When young Apache girls reached the age of womanhood, she was to see that they were feted with a proper celebration. The ceremony was to include only the chaste girls, their relatives, and the holy men and women of the tribe. The celebration was to commemorate the sacredness and importance of the gift of producing life and was to last four days and nights. The holy men and women were to pray and sing for the young women while others pounded on the drums. The girls were to dance in a circle around the medicine men and women, and outside of this assemblage the rest of the tribe would dance in the opposite direction.

This ceremony was intended to insure the future of the tribe, and with little variation is still practiced today.

Even though the United States Army cavalry eventually drove the Apaches from the Guadalupe Mountains and onto reservations, there beats in the breast of every living Mescalero today the hope that they may someday return to their homeland and live a life of peace and harmony, good hunting, and successful raiding. Here they will grow strong sons and healthy daughters who will help them rule this rugged environment as they once did.

To that end, the ghosts of the ancestors continue to perform their ceremony in the shadow of El Capitan Peak.

Chapter Three

The Village of the Dead

DEEP IN MCKITTRICK CANYON in the Guadalupe Mountains, an 1851 military reconnaissance party encountered an entire encampment of Indians stricken by some mysterious death. Skeletons and shriveled corpses of thirty-five Apaches—men, women, and children—lay upon the ground in a manner suggesting they all met their end at the same time and under the same bizarre circumstances. Subsequent examination of the remains revealed no signs of violence, and the curious deaths remain a mystery to this day.

In 1851, Richard Irving Dodge was a young officer in charge of a U.S. Army cavalry unit. Assigned to southern New Mexico and the Trans-Pecos area of Texas, Lieutenant Dodge and his command were given the responsibility of protecting settlers and travelers from depredations by Mescalero Apaches and Comanches who roamed this region. Since the Mescaleros lived in the Guadalupe

Mountains, the range was visited often by Dodge as he sought to make contact with the Indians.

Following raids on area ranches and small settlements throughout much of West Texas, southern New Mexico, and Mexico, the Mescaleros returned to the Guadalupe Mountains with herds of stolen cattle and horses along with a number of captives. While following the tracks of the stolen livestock was a relatively easy task for the cavalry, overtaking the raiders and engaging them in combat proved to be more difficult. On entering the Guadalupes, Dodge would often discover the Indians had simply fled through the range toward the north and into the Sacramento Mountains. On the few occasions Dodge and his troopers were able to engage the Mescaleros in a skirmish, the Indians would attack suddenly and from a variety of hiding places and then quickly melt into the dense forests of the high country, leaving the soldiers alone and bewildered.

During the summer of 1851, Lieutenant Dodge led a small scouting party into the Guadalupe Mountains in search of the Mescalero's campground. Their orders were to attack the camp, confiscate the livestock, and burn the lodges and captured articles. As they crossed ridges and explored valleys and canyons throughout the vast range, Dodge and his soldiers encountered abundant game, numerous springs, and a great many hiding places, an environment quite suitable, he thought, for the Apache.

During this expedition, one of Dodge's scouts came upon an Indian trail that led downward into a steep-walled canyon. The path was deep and wide and at one time must have accommodated a great deal of traffic, but there was no indication it had been used for several years. Curious, Dodge decided to follow it.

The trail wound gradually downward across the flank of a

portion of the range, leading the soldiers into an area of dense forest. Wary of ambush, Dodge proceeded cautiously. Presently, the trail leveled out into the upper reaches of a beautiful canyon. From Dodge's description, it could only have been South McKittrick Canyon. Here, a stream of cool, clear water sparkled in the afternoon sunlight and offered needed refreshment for men and horses alike.

After calling a halt, Dodge regarded the sheer cliffs that rose hundreds of feet high on each side of the valley, the only entrance and exit being the trail which they followed. Along the valley floor as far as Dodge could see, thick groves of trees grew along the bank of the stream.

Over twenty-five years later, Dodge wrote of his experience in a book titled *The Hunting Grounds of the Great West*. In his book, Dodge described the stream as beautiful, and wrote that it "wound in graceful curves from mountain to mountain as if seeking to leave no spot of the valley untouched by its invigorating influence." Between clusters of trees, "smooth lawns of the greenest grass, dotted with clumps of shrubbery, and covered with lovely flowers of every hue, made a picture as fair as the eye of man could wish it." As Dodge wrote about this cool and protected setting, he stated that it had a resort-like, almost paradisical feeling to it, suggesting it must have been a favorite resting place for the Mescalero Apaches.

Following a brief rest during which the troopers and horses drank their fill, Dodge, leading the column, continued along the trail as it paralleled the stream to lower levels of the canyon. After traveling about three or four miles over country which Dodge described as "a most charming valley, nestled and hidden in the very bosom of the mountains . . . ," he noted the canyon floor growing wider and more lush. Tracks of deer, bear, and mountain lion could be seen in the soft soil near the banks of the stream. Sounds of animals moving through the brush and trees could be heard. As the troopers marveled at this pleasant setting, their reverie was broken by the sudden appearance of one of the advance scouts who rode up and informed Dodge of the presence of an Indian village a short distance ahead.

As Dodge turned to order his troopers to check their weapons and prepare for hostile contact, the scout told the lieutenant that all of the Indians in the village were dead!

Proceeding cautiously along the floor of the canyon, the soldiers rode in the protection of the trees. After rounding a bend in the valley, they came into view of the Indian campground. The first thing they noticed was a number of lodges that had fallen to the mercy of wind and rain—coverings were blown off or had rotted away. Here and there about the campground they saw corroded cooking utensils lying near what apparently had once been campfires. Rotted saddles were perched next to the dwellings. Weapons that appeared to have been in the process of being cleaned were lying on the ground where their owners must have set them down. From all appearances, it seemed as though the camp had been suddenly abandoned and everything left where it was.

As the troopers rode into the strangely quiet uninhabited camp, Dodge and the riders at the head of the column reined in their horses. There, scattered across the ground before them, were the skeletons and shriveled corpses of thirty Indians. To Dodge, it seemed as if each of the occupants of the camp simply fell dead where they were standing or sitting.

Dismounting, Dodge examined several of the remains. As he went from corpse to corpse and skeleton to skeleton, he could detect no sign of violence whatsoever—no visible wounds, no scalping, nothing. "To all appearances," wrote Dodge, "not a thing had been touched by man . . . [and] not a living soul had entered that camp since the day of its awful visitation by the bad god."

A subsequent count by Dodge revealed thirty-five Indians died, and it appeared as though every one of them had suddenly dropped dead.

The strange case of what has been called the Mescalero Village of the Dead was never solved. During subsequent interviews with captured Indians, Dodge was never able to gain any information relative to what had befallen the unlucky Apache residents of McKittrick Canyon.

To this day, the mystery remains unsolved.

Chapter Four

Killed, Buried, Dug Up, and Scalped!

A SHORT DISTANCE from paved Highway 62–180 as it winds up the western slope of Guadalupe Pass lies a solitary grave. The crudely marked slab of limestone set vertically at the head of the grave identifies it as:

Jose Maria Polanco
Guide
Killed Feb.
1855
by Indians

Polanco, a guide for infantry Captain James Longstreet, met his death at the hands of Mescalero Apaches and was buried at this location by the soldiers. A day later, however, Polanco's body was disinterred, scalped, mutilated, and shot full of arrows by the Indians.

Jose Maria Polanco, believed to be half Indian and half Mexican, signed on as guide for Longstreet's 8th Infantry near Hueco Tanks, a cluster of igneous intrusive knobs about forty miles east of Fort Bliss, Texas. No one knows where Polanco came from, and his life prior to his arrival at Hueco Tanks remains a mystery. After taking the job as guide, Polanco's life lasted only eight more days.

Polanco's assignment was to guide Longstreet's command of fifty-four troops, along with several wagons filled with supplies and ammunition, into the Guadalupe Mountains. The command was scheduled to travel across the desert and into the mountain range for reconnaissance, and Polanco, riding a horse from the detachment's remuda, led the soldiers along the easiest and safest trails. For the next few days, Polanco proved to be a competent guide and was often seen conversing and joking with the troopers.

On approaching Crow Springs near the western escarpment of the mountains, Polanco, who had been ranging far ahead of the unit, informed Longstreet that a group of Indians were watering a herd of about forty head of cattle at the springs. Suspecting the cattle were stolen, Longstreet gathered his lieutenants about him and made plans to attack the Indians, but by the time the soldiers reached the springs, the renegades had departed and were seen in the distance herding the livestock toward Guadalupe Pass.

Longstreet selected Polanco to lead a detachment of twelve troopers to follow the Indians. Once in the mountains, they were to try to determine the strength of the Indian force as well as the location of their camp and report back. Several hours later, a hard-riding soldier from the scouting party galloped his lathered horse into camp to inform Longstreet that the Indians were last seen watering the cattle at Guadalupe Spring near the foothills of El Capitan Peak. Longstreet ordered the rest of his men to mount up, and moments later they were on the trail toward Guadalupe Pass.

When Longstreet and the rest of the command arrived at Guadalupe Spring, Polanco and the scouting party were waiting for them. The Indians, presumed to be Mescalero Apaches, had herded the cattle up into the higher reaches of the range only moments earlier.

As the soldiers established a camp near the spring, Longstreet instructed Polanco to follow the Indians' trail up into the mountains, assess their strength, and report back as soon as possible. Taking only his rifle, Polanco, on foot, began climbing the slope adjacent to the steep, winding, and rocky trail.

Unknown to Longstreet or Polanco, about two dozen Apaches were at that moment creeping down the mountain on foot. Their intention was to attack the soldiers at dawn the following day. Polanco, cautiously and quietly making his way up the side of the mountain in the darkness, came face to face with the advancing Indians. Both the guide and the Mescaleros were startled. Realizing he had no chance in a fight with the Indians, Polanco turned to flee down the mountainside back to the camp. At the same time, the Indians let loose a volley of arrows, at least seven of which pierced the body of the unfortunate guide, killing him instantly.

Fearing that other scouts might be searching this part of the range, the Indians abandoned their plans to attack and retreated back up the slope.

On the afternoon of the following day, Polanco's body was found by the soldiers. After returning the dead man to the camp, Longstreet ordered the body be transported some distance down the trail and given a suitable burial. While that was being done, Longstreet moved his command from Guadalupe Spring to Pine Spring, about one mile to the east where firewood was more plentiful.

Three days later, a scouting party led by Major Simonson arrived at Longstreet's Pine Spring encampment. After exchanging pleasantries, Simonson informed Longstreet that earlier in the day he had passed a fresh gravesite. According to the major, a body of what appeared to be a Mexican had been dug up, all the clothes removed from it, and the scalp taken. In addition, said Simonson, the body was mutilated and shot full of arrows. After removing the arrows and wrapping the body in a blanket, Simonson's men reburied it.

Why the Indians took the trouble to disinter the body and desecrate it was a mystery to Longstreet and Simonson as well as to researchers who encountered references to it in Longstreet's journals. Years later, an explanation was advanced by Santos Barza, a Mescalero Apache. Barza claimed that at some period prior to joining Longstreet's command as a guide, Polanco lived with the Mescaleros in the Guadalupe Mountains. Barza, who believed Polanco was probably the offspring of an Apache warrior and a Mexican woman, either deserted the tribe or was banished for some misdeed. Barza believed that digging up a body to scalp it and fill it full of arrows was an act of revenge reserved for only the worst of traitors or those disloyal to the Apaches.

Whatever Polanco did to deserve such treatment in death will never be known, but his gravesite near the modern-day highway is a reminder of the dangers that were once so common in this mountain range. Captain Longstreet would go on to fame as a confederate general during the Civil War. Acting as a lieutenant to Robert E. Lee he would take part in many of the major battles of that conflict.

Chapter Five

≈|≈

The Lost Gold Mine of Ben Sublett

THE YEAR WAS 1881, and a prospector named William Colwell Sublett may have accidentally discovered a long lost secret gold mine of the Mescalero Apaches in the Guadalupe Mountains. The fifty-year-old Sublett, whose life was fraught with hardship and difficulty, returned time and again to the mine to retrieve the precious ore. He even directed others to it, but today its location remains one of the greatest mysteries of the range. According to some researchers, the gold mine, if it exists, may be one of the richest in America.

Growing up in Tennessee, Sublett became a drifter at an early age, going from one job to another and never remaining very long at any of them. For a time, he served with the Texas Rangers, and in 1862 he joined the Confederate army. After Lee's surrender in 1865, Sublett mustered out of the military, and his subsequent wanderings took him to Arkansas where he married Laura Louise Denney. During the next several years, the couple gradually moved

FIG. 4 William Colwell Sublett.
(PHOTO COURTESY DANA KIRK WITMER.)

westward in search of a healthier climate for Laura, who suffered from tuberculosis. In the meantime, three children were born.

By the mid-1870s, the Sublett family had arrived in the Trans-Pecos region of West Texas. By the time they reached the small settlement of Monahans, they were out of money and nearly out of food. After setting up housekeeping on the outskirts of town in the back of their wagon and in an old shabby tent, Sublett worked at odd jobs while Laura and the oldest daughter took in washing.

When Sublett wasn't whitewashing buildings or mopping out saloons, he took occasional prospecting trips into the Guadalupe Mountains about one hundred miles to the west. Though others warned of the presence of hostile Apaches in the range, Sublett went anyway.

Because of his predilection for ignoring the ever-present danger of the warring Apaches, and because of his eccentric behavior, his inability to hold a job for long, and his unkempt appearance, Sublett was regarded by many Monahans citizens as a bit crazy, a reputation that seemed not to bother him at all.

Often thought of as just another demented prospector lured by the promise of wealth and having spent too much time in the broiling West Texas sun, Sublett was soon nicknamed Old Ben. Children made fun of him, and area residents, feeling sorry for his family, grew accustomed to giving him small handouts when jobs were few and far between.

Eventually, Old Ben moved his family to Odessa, a larger town some twenty-five miles to the northeast. Odessa was a growing center of economic and ranching activity, and while still very much a wild west town, it provided a more suitable climate in which to raise children. Old Ben was also hopeful of finding greater opportunities for employment.

Not long after the move to Odessa, Laura Sublett died, and Old Ben had to look after his three children alone. Unfortunately, the reputation he garnered in Monahans followed him to the larger town, and as a result of his usual decrepit appearance, along with his oft-repaired wagon pulled by two ill-fed mules, he continued to be the target of cruel jokes and found jobs as difficult to obtain as before.

Occasionally leaving his children in the care of neighbors, Sublett continued to make prospecting forays into the Guadalupe Mountains, and promised any who would listen to him that he would soon strike it rich.

The lure of potential wealth in this wild range of mountains was powerful for Sublett, and it continued to pull at him, drawing him to its deep, dark canyons and rocky ridges. The massive limestone formations and the shaded valleys of the Guadalupes never suggested the existence of gold or any other kind of valuable ore lying in the aged and crumbling beds of sedimentary rock, but Old Ben continued to search, often spending weeks at a time in the range.

In spite of the presence of Indians, Sublett always returned to Odessa with his scalp intact, but his repeated visits to the savage environs served to enhance his reputation as a crazy man.

Once, when Sublett was employed to whitewash the exterior of an Odessa saloon, he met an old Apache Indian. Like Old Ben, the Indian was down on his luck and lived a hand-to-mouth existence with odd jobs and handouts. During a break one afternoon, the Apache told Old Ben he knew the secret location of a rich gold mine in the Guadalupe Mountains.

Intrigued, Sublett pressed the old man for details and learned enough to construct a crude map of the location. Following that encounter, Old Ben's trips to the Guadalupes grew more frequent, and his quest to locate the mine grew into an obsession.

Sublett's continued and sustained searches for the Guadalupe gold had the immediate effect of neglecting his children, and soon their only income was that taken in by the oldest daughter from washing clothes. Eventually, some of the town's leading citizens expressed concern for the welfare of the children and called for authorities to take them away from the crazy prospector and place them in homes where they could be properly cared for.

While his children were the subject of discussion in Odessa, Sublett was busy searching for gold in the Guadalupes. Using the map he made from the description provided by the Indian, Old Ben found himself in a shallow canyon or ravine on the southeast-facing slope of the range not far from Manzanilla Spring, certain he was close to the gold. As he made his way between shallow potholes filled with water from a recent rain, he searched for some sign of the precious metal, ever hopeful of discovery.

And then it happened.

In negotiating his way up the deep ravine, Sublett was suddenly distracted by a glint from something on the ground. On stooping to examine it, his heart thudded in his chest when he discovered it was a gold nugget.

Dropping to his hands and knees, Sublett raked his fingers through the gravel that lined the canyon floor and moments later found three more gold nuggets, each one as large as a ladybug. During the next hour, Old Ben retrieved over a dozen more nuggets.

As he slowly made his way up the ravine, Sublett observed that the quantity of gold nuggets increased. Up ahead, he surmised, he would find the source of the ore, the mother lode, and moments later he did.

In a minute outcrop of dark intrusive rock on one side of the ravine, Sublett spotted a low, narrow entrance to a mine shaft. Stooping, he crawled in and examined it as far as the penetrating daylight would permit. He crawled back out, fashioned a makeshift torch from some tough grasses he found nearby, and reentered. At the end of the deep, steeply slanted shaft, Sublett recounted in later years, he found a thick vein of gold, the metal so soft that it was easily cut with a knife. On the floor of the shaft at his feet, nuggets were scattered about in profusion, most of them quite large.

William Colwell Sublett had finally struck it rich.

One week later, Sublett pulled his creaky wagon up to the front of Odessa's Mollie Williams Saloon. Walking inside, he loudly ordered drinks for everyone and dumped out a buckskin pouch full of gold nuggets onto the bar. When all of the saloon's patrons approached to stare at the incredible fortune in gold, Old Ben announced that he had just found the richest gold mine in all America.

Sublett, once considered by many to be little more than a bum, was now a wealthy celebrity in Odessa. The day immediately following his return, he sought for and located proper accommodations for his three children, outfitted them with new clothes, and enrolled them in school. Life had finally taken a positive turn for Old Ben.

Three weeks later and after a number of purchases, Sublett found himself running low on funds and began making plans for another trip into the mountains. On numerous occasions thereafter, Old Ben disappeared into the Guadalupes for days at a time, always returning with two or three pouches filled with gold. Acquaintances who saw the ore described it as being very pure.

Several Odessa citizens burned with curiosity to learn the

location of Sublett's secret mine. Some even offered him large amounts of money to take them to it, but Old Ben remained aloof and guarded, reminding them that it was only a short time ago they were all saying he was crazy.

Sublett was often followed when he left Odessa for the Guadalupes. Expecting such tactics, he would sometimes go to elaborate lengths to throw trackers off his trail. He departed at odd hours of the night. He would set up camp on the Pecos River, remain for three or four days, and return to Odessa. Sometimes he would simply elude those who tried to follow, arriving in town several days later with more gold.

Old Ben kept his money in a Midland bank owned by one W. E. Connell. Connell noticed that whenever Sublett's account ran low he would make another trip to the mountains. Within a week, Sublett returned to Midland and invariably deposited a lot of cash. Connell could never determine where Sublett exchanged his gold for cash, and to this day no one has solved this mystery.

Connell, along with Midland rancher George Gray, approached Sublett one day with an offer of ten thousand dollars for his rich gold mine. Old Ben responded with a laugh along with the comment that, in less than a week's time he could pick up that much and more in gold. The response infuriated Connell and Gray, and over the next several weeks they plotted to find the mine for themselves.

Connell and Gray hired a local man named Jim Flannigan to track Sublett to his mine and report back to them. Once, when Old Ben's account ran low, Flannigan was notified that a trip to the mountains was imminent. Lee Driver, owner of a Midland livery stable and an accomplice of Connell and Gray, kept a horse ready for Flannigan to use at a moment's notice. Following two weeks of patient waiting, Gray spotted Sublett leaving Odessa in a carriage pulled by two burros and followed his tracks, remaining out of sight about two miles behind.

Sublett's carriage tracks were easy to spot in the soft West Texas sand that covers much of the Trans-Pecos region, and Flannigan had no trouble following the prospector for nearly seventy-five miles. Somewhere along the trail where it paralleled the Pecos River, Sublett eluded his tracker.

Frantic, Flannigan circled the area several times trying to find some trace of the carriage tracks but had no luck. On returning to Odessa, he discovered Sublett had beat him back and already deposited a large amount of money in Connell's bank.

Sublett did not have many friends, but one man with whom he often shared time was an old prospector who went by the name of Grizzly Bill. Once, while the two were out deer hunting, Old Ben revealed the location of his mine, telling Bill that it contained more gold than he could ever use and that he wanted to share it with someone.

Weeks later, Grizzly Bill, following Sublett's directions, apparently found the mine. Unable to contain his excitement, Bill stopped at a tavern in Pecos to show off his new-found riches and initiated a celebration that lasted for two days. The old prospector drank more liquor than he was able to hold, and found himself talked into a bronc-riding contest. During the ride, Bill was thrown from the horse and died instantly from a broken neck.

Sublett shared the location of his mine with another man named Mike Wilson. Having been friends with Wilson for a number of years, Old Ben gave him directions for finding it. After locating the mine and filling several pouches with gold nuggets, Wilson returned to Odessa and, like Grizzly Bill, threw a party. Three days later after Wilson sobered up he discovered all of his gold was gone, so he decided to take another trip into the Guadalupes.

During his second trip to the mountains, Wilson became disoriented and confused and was unable to remember the directions provided by his friend. He returned to Odessa and sought out Old Ben for help, but Sublett was so disgusted with Wilson's carelessness that he refused to talk to him. Mike Wilson spent the better part of the remainder of his life searching for the rich gold mine he had found and lost.

During the 1880s, a man named Rufus Stewart was often seen in the Trans-Pecos area. Sometimes Stewart worked as a guide for immigrants traveling westward. In 1888, Stewart, who knew the favorite feeding grounds of antelope and deer in the region, was employed by the Texas and Pacific Railroad to guide several company officials on an antelope hunt near the Pecos River.

Late one night in camp after the railroad men had gone to sleep, Stewart was checking on the horses when he heard the sound of an approaching wagon. Moments later the driver came into view, pulled up to the blazing campfire, and stepped down. Stewart immediately recognized the newcomer as Old Ben Sublett whom he had known for years. Stewart was aware of the stories of Sublett's gold mine, but never believed any of them.

After offering Sublett some coffee, Stewart and Old Ben sat around the campfire in conversation. Looking around to make certain no one was listening, Sublett confided to Stewart he was on his way to his gold mine in the Guadalupe Mountains. He also told him this would probably be his last trip as he was getting on in years and possessed all the gold he would ever need. Sublett told Stewart that if he would go with him, he would show him the location of the mine.

Stewart, not entirely believing Sublett, responded that he could not leave the men he had been entrusted to guide. He also confessed to having some concerns about entering Apache territory. Sublett told Stewart that the Apaches would never bother him as long as he, Sublett, accompanied him into the range. Though tempted, Stewart decided to remain in camp.

The following morning, Stewart prepared a large breakfast for the hunters and shared it with Sublett. As Old Ben readied his wagon and horses, Stewart told him he would ride along with him for a short distance. Later, the two men paused atop what Stewart later described as a "blue mound" located west of the camp. From here, Sublett pointed toward the Guadalupe Mountains and gave Stewart directions relative to reaching the gold mine. The two men shook hands and Sublett promised he would stop to visit on his return trip in three days.

True to his word, Sublett arrived in the hunters' camp on the evening of the third day. When the railroad men finally crawled into their bedrolls for the night, Sublett waved Stewart over to the light of the campfire. After unrolling a piece of buckskin, Sublett opened a leather pouch and from it poured a quantity of gold nuggets. Stewart remarked that all of the nuggets appeared to be uncommonly large, and Old Ben replied that the large ones are simply easier to pick up than the smaller ones, and that each time he ran his hands through the gravel he would uncover more of the big ones.

Several weeks later, Stewart, using Sublett's directions, attempted to locate the rich mine in the Guadalupes, but could not find it.

Sublett was known to share the secret location of his gold mine with only one other person, his son Rolth. Years after Old

Ben died, Rolth made several attempts to locate the gold, but was never successful.

For the remainder of his life, Old Ben Sublett lived comfortably on the gold he claimed he dug from his secret mine in the mountains. At the time of his death in 1892, his fortune was nearly exhausted and he did not leave much of an inheritance. More than anyone else associated with the Guadalupe Mountains, however, William Colwell Sublett left a fascinating legacy.

That Sublett found gold in the Guadalupes has never been in doubt, and to this day hundreds of fortune hunters arrive in the range each year to search for the source.

Most researchers believe that Sublett's gold and the Apache gold are the same. The notion has also been advanced that Old Ben may have participated in holdups of mail and freight wagons traveling between El Paso and points east, and that the gold was from booty taken during these robberies. Others opine that Sublett may have found a cache left from an earlier robbery. This, however, is pure conjecture, and there is no evidence to support the contention.

Today, a large portion of the Guadalupe Mountains lies within the boundaries of a national park, and treasure hunting is forbidden by law. The lure of Sublett's gold remains powerful, however, and many continue to dream of finding it. They arrive in the Guadalupe Mountains, each sincerely believing he will be the one to locate the famous mine.

Chapter Six

The Saga of Rolth Sublett

As a NINE-YEAR-OLD child in 1887, Rolth Sublett once accompanied his father, Old Ben Sublett, to one of the most famous lost mines in the history of the West—the Lost Sublett Mine of the Guadalupe Mountains.

During the trip, Rolth, unconcerned about the significance of his father's discovery, amused himself for several days with a bear cub he found. While Old Ben removed several pounds of gold from his secret location, Rolth played with his new pet.

Time and again, Old Ben lowered himself, along with several canteens full of water, into a deep rock crevice. Just before disappearing over the edge of the opening, he always checked on the whereabouts of his son. Rolth was always close by and helpful when needed, but the distractions of this day left him unconcerned about the fabulous wealth in gold being taken from the bottom of the crevice, and he gave no thought whatsoever to the location of the mine. Rolth spent most of his adult life regretting his lack of concern.

When Rolth was fourteen, Old Ben lay dying on a hospital bed in Odessa, Texas. Rolth and his sisters gathered at the bedside of their father. By this time, the importance of the location of the mine had become clear to Rolth, and he knelt next to his father and begged him to reveal the location of the secret mine. Old Ben, his voice barely audible above his rasping breath, told his son that any description he could provide would be useless. Just before he died, Sublett pulled his son close and told him he would just have to go out into the mountains and find the mine for himself. Rolth spent the rest of his life doing just that.

After Old Ben died, what was left of the savings he had spent many years and a great deal of effort accumulating was gradually used up by his family. As they began to fall on hard times, Rolth decided to try to find the source of his father's gold on his own.

During the next fifty years, Rolth Sublett traveled to the Guadalupe Mountains hundreds of times in search of the Lost Sublett Mine. Finding the location of his father's gold obsessed the younger Sublett, consumed him, and dominated his every thought and conversation. Some who knew Rolth well claimed it drove him just crazy enough to neglect everything else—his family, his job, his friends. Those who knew Old Ben stated they saw a lot of the father in the eccentric ways of the son.

Like his father, Rolth was a born salesman and possessed an impressive power to persuade. As a result, he located a number of financial backers so that he might devote his full time and effort to the search. Each trip into the mountains, however, ended in failure and temporary discouragement.

When he was an old man, Rolth told Texas folklorist J. Frank Dobie that his father's gold was located at the bottom of a deep, wide, crevice. The location was a two-day wagon ride from a crossing on the Pecos River and in a canyon of the south- or southeast-facing slope of the Guadalupe Mountains. The only way into it, said Rolth, was by rope ladder. Rolth told others that his father always carried two or three canteens with him. The water was used to wash the gold ore from the dirt and debris at the bottom of the crevice.

On one occasion, Old Ben tied a rope around Rolth and lowered him into the opening, but the boy was more interested in returning to the surface and playing with his bear cub than he was in the dark and frightening interior of the deep crack.

As Rolth grew to manhood he moved to Carlsbad, New Mexico, and supported himself much as his father had when he first arrived in the West. When he ran low on money, he worked at odd jobs just long enough to acquire enough funds to travel to the Guadalupes to search for his father's lost mine. For a time, Rolth worked in the bat guano mines that eventually became Carlsbad Caverns National Park.

The late Walter and Bertha Glover, early settlers and long-time residents of Pine Springs, knew Rolth well. They recalled Rolth arriving in the mountains many times, always stopping at the Glover's Pine Springs Café to visit. According to Bertha, Rolth always arrived in a broken-down horse-drawn wagon and was sometimes accompanied by a grubstaker. Rolth always referred to his partner as a "financial backer," but Walter Glover referred to him as "just another sucker for one of Rolth's lost mine schemes."

The Glovers, while fond of Rolth, never believed in the existence of the Lost Sublett Mine. They were convinced, however, that Rolth earned a decent, if somewhat dishonest, living by conning others into investing in its discovery and development.

Bertha Glover recalled that Rolth and whatever backer was with him at the time would normally camp for four or five days near the mouth of Pine Spring Canyon. During the day, the two men would search the southeast-facing slope from Pine Spring to Rader Ridge about five miles to the northeast.

Rolth told several people that he believed the lost mine was located in Rustler Hills, some forty miles east of El Capitan Peak, yet he always confined his own searches to the vicinity of the Guadalupe Mountains. Some were convinced Rolth told the Rustler Hills story to throw searchers off track.

The late Ben Wattson, a sometime resident of Pine Springs and part-time employee of Walter Glover, recalled searching for the lost mine with Rolth on several occasions, even working for the younger Sublett as cook as the trade demanded. Wattson, who claimed to have known Old Ben, described Rolth as "a short man but wiry and muscular, with salt-and-pepper hair that turned gray at an early age." Wattson said Rolth always wore calf-high cowboy boots with his britches tucked into the tops in the manner of the cowhands of the day who worked in the area. Rolth possessed a great deal of energy, according to Wattson, and never seemed to tire from the day-long searches in the front range of the mountains.

A few who have researched the legend of the Lost Sublett Mine are unconvinced that such a lode ever existed. Many others, however, claim there can be no doubt there was such a deposit of gold. The believers cite Rolth's personal experience with the mine and his dozens of expeditions into the mountains in search of it. It is true that Rolth had financial backing for many of the trips, but he often arrived in the range to search by himself and at his own expense.

Some skeptics claim Rolth parlayed the tale of his father's gold into a money-making business by convincing investors to finance his searches. Those who knew him well agree that he was a bit eccentric, but that he was a man of integrity and would not stoop to conning people into investing in a nonexistent gold mine.

Ben Wattson was convinced the mine existed. He said he spent many an evening seated at a campfire with the younger Sublett listening to him telling stories about his father and the mine. Wattson, a pauper for most of his life and completely unable to finance a treasure-hunting operation himself, said Rolth had no reason to try to con him into believing the story if it wasn't true.

Based on the many conversations he claimed he had with Rolth, Wattson believed the elusive rock crevice from which Old Ben brought forth a fortune in gold was located somewhere between Pine Spring and Rader Ridge. Wattson also surmised that the site was probably covered by a landslide during the early 1900s. He was convinced he knew the exact location of the lost crevice, but could not afford the men or equipment it would require to remove the rock debris.

As Rolth grew older, his trips to the Guadalupe Mountains became less frequent. Advancing age and infirmities aggravated by arthritis slowed his movement through the steep, rocky canyons and slopes of the range. Eventually, Rolth settled in Artesia, New Mexico, and it was said he became a prominent businessman. Years passed, and Rolth grew weaker with back problems and found himself unable to return to the Guadalupe Mountains to search for his father's famous lost mine. Though bedridden in his later years, Rolth never tired of relating tales of his experience searching for the gold. He stuck to his conviction that the mine did exist and that someday he would find it.

Unfortunately, Rolth never found the source of his father's gold. Weakened by pneumonia, he died and was buried in Artesia.

Though Rolth Sublett is gone, the search for the Lost Sublett

Mine continues, now more than ever. During the years since Rolth's death, several significant caches of what are believed to be stolen ore have been discovered along the front range of the Guadalupe Mountains, undoubtedly the spoil of robberies. Some researchers believe Old Ben was retrieving ore from one or more of these caches, but Rolth maintained that his father carried water down into the mine to wash the gold from the gravel at the bottom of a deep crevice.

Though history has recorded that Old Ben Sublett did indeed find gold, the wealth represented by that ore eluded Rolth his entire life. Knowing that it existed, having actually seen it but never being able to relocate it, tortured Rolth for as long as he lived.

As Rolth grew older, he grew more philosophical. He once commented that he was probably never meant to find the gold, and that maybe if he had it would have brought him nothing but trouble. Rolth confessed that he never had much luck managing what money he did have.

Rolth once stated that he was sorry that his passion for finding his father's gold caused him to miss enjoying a normal life. He had very few close friends, and many people avoided him because they were convinced he was crazy. It was the same kind of fate his father was forced to endure during much of his own lifetime.

Whatever else he was, Rolth Sublett was a central figure in one of the greatest treasure legends of all time.

Chapter Seven

Apache Gold

GERONIMO, THE FAMOUS medicine man and warrior of the Bedonkohe Apaches, once said the Guadalupe Mountains were the source of all the gold used by the Indians. When Geronimo finally surrendered to General Nelson Miles in 1886, he was sent to prison and placed under heavy guard. Once, while attempting to bargain for his release, Geronimo told his captors that if they let him go he would take them to the Guadalupes and show them so much gold that, as he claimed, it would take a company of soldiers to carry it all away. The location of this vast treasure, said Geronimo, was a secret known only to the Apaches.

Though thousands have searched, very few white men have ever seen the gold of the Guadalupes. One of the men who spent a great deal of time, energy, and money searching for the legendary wealth was a San Antonio chiropractor who learned of it from one of his patients.

The year was 1926, and the citizens of San Antonio were sweltering in one of the hottest summers in memory. During midday, residents sought the relatively cool shade of live oak trees in the downtown park. It is unlikely that any of those seated at the park benches noticed as an aged Mexican haltingly made his way along a nearby sidewalk. With considerable difficulty, the old man paused often to read the addresses on buildings he passed and checked them against a notation on a crumpled sheet of paper he held between his weathered fingers. Eventually, he found the office for which he searched, folded and pocketed the piece of paper, and entered. It was the office of a chiropractor.

Clutching his ragged hat with both hands, the old man walked up to the receptionist, told her his name was Polycarpio Gonzalez, and that he was deaf. He asked her if she thought the chiropractor could help him.

An hour later, Polycarpio was admitted to the chiropractor's office. After being seated, he told of his deafness and that he had seen many doctors in the past but none were able to help. He said his daughter suggested the chiropractor and gave him the name of the man standing before him. All he wanted to do, said Polycarpio, was to hear music once again.

Employing a crude sign language on the spot, the chiropractor told the old man he would try to help, and during the next several weeks he undertook a series of treatments.

As summer gradually faded to autumn, Polycarpio continued visiting the chiropractor's office once every two weeks. One day as the old Mexican was leaving the doctor's office, he politely requested permission to rest for a while in the waiting room. It was a long way to his daughter's house, he said, and he was very tired. While Polycarpio was seated in a comfortable chair, the receptionist turned on a radio. Suddenly, Polycarpio's eyes opened wide. A moment later, he straightened up and began shouting that he could hear the music. Excited, he rose from the chair and shuffled across the floor in a strange dance. The chiropractor, on hearing the noise, came to investigate.

After several minutes of dancing, the old Mexican grew exhausted and collapsed into the chair. As Polycarpio recovered his breath, the doctor approached and inquired about the unusual style of dancing he had just performed, remarking that it was a kind unknown to him. Polycarpio breathlessly replied that he learned the dance from the Apaches. In his excitement to rush home and tell his daughter he was able to hear, he rose from the chair, excused himself, and proceeded out the door and down the street.

One week later, Polycarpio Gonzalez returned to the chiropractor's office and requested a meeting with him. After being ushered into an office, the Mexican expressed his gratitude to the doctor for restoring his hearing. He told him he was now able to spend many pleasant hours each day listening to the wonderful music he had missed for so long. With some embarrassment, Polycarpio also told the doctor he had very little money with which to pay for his treatment, but wished to make an offer of something else. When asked what it was, Polycarpio related the most amazing story the doctor had ever heard.

When Polycarpio was four years old, his mother gave him to a cavalry officer named Colonel Boone. Boone was a noted Indian fighter and, at the time, stationed at Fort Stockton, Texas. A competent officer and veteran of many Indian skirmishes, Boone was given the assignment of protecting travelers and settlers from raiding Apaches.

FIG. 5 Apache warriors.
(PHOTO COURTESY NATIONAL PARK SERVICE.)

Young Polycarpio was sometimes permitted to accompany the soldiers on scouting missions, and one evening found him riding with thirteen troopers far south of the fort and near the Mexican border. As it grew dark, the soldiers decided to make camp near a rocky ravine when they were suddenly attacked by about fifty Mescalero Apaches. A violent and bloody battle ensued and all of the troopers were slain. Polycarpio was struck in the leg by a bullet and was crawling into some nearby brush to hide when the Indians saw him. Consistent with Apache custom, the youth was taken and raised as one of their own.

Polycarpio lived with the Apaches for fourteen years. He willingly learned what they taught, and in time became a competent warrior among what many consider to be the greatest fighters in history. He claimed the Indians were always kind to him, taught him their language, shared everything they owned, and showed him how to dance the Mescalero way.

During certain times of the year, the Mescaleros camped near Manzanita Spring near the southern slope of the Guadalupe escarpment. Here, the women would harvest the abundant mescal plants and prepare stores for the winter. The men, when not hunting, remained in camp cleaning rifles, making arrows, and talking of battles with the white soldiers.

While camped at Manzanita Spring, Polycarpio was taken into confidence by one of the elders and told that nearby was the source of the gold the Apaches used to fashion their ornaments and sometimes traded for weapons and ammunition. The gold, continued the elder, was once mined by ancestors under the supervision of a race of mounted white warriors who came from the north. The newcomers, believed to be Spaniards, remained in the Guadalupe Mountains until a great drought drove them away.

FIG. 6 Arroyo that contains lost Apache gold mine.
(PHOTO COURTESY LAURIE WAGNER BUYER.)

The following morning, the elder invited Polycarpio to accompany him to the location of the secret gold. Some of the ore was needed, he said, to trade for weapons. The two walked along the rim of a nearby ravine until the elder stopped and pointed to a jumble of rocks at the bottom. There, Polycarpio was told, was where the mine shaft was located.

Polycarpio and the elder slid down the steep slope of the ravine and stood among the boulders. Displaying a strength belying his age, the elder rolled aside several of the larger rocks, exposing the opening to a tunnel that extended into an outcrop of solid granite at a steep angle. From behind another rock, the elder withdrew a

FIG. 7 Manzanita Spring.
(PHOTO COURTESY LAURIE WAGNER BUYER.)

length of rope. After securing the rope to a nearby juniper, he lit a grass torch and proceeded to lower himself into the sloping shaft. Polycarpio followed.

It was eighty feet to the end of the tunnel, and here the elder showed the young man how to carve pieces of the soft yellow metal from the sinuous veins of white quartz that snaked through the rock. The shaft, which followed the gold-laced quartz vein, was evidently dug by hand and bore the marks of picks and hand-held drills. Lying about the floor at the terminus of the shaft were several leather pouches, each one filled with gold. The elder retrieved one of the pouches and, together, the two climbed out.

The following morning at sunrise, a scout rode into camp and informed the chief of an approaching company of cavalry, still a day or two away. The chief called the tribe together, told them they could no longer remain at the spring since it was not defensible, and gave the order to break camp. Turning to the elder, he gave instructions to fill the mine shaft so the whites would not find the gold of the Apaches. The elder, along with Polycarpio and several other young braves, proceeded to the ravine and rolled rocks and boulders into the shaft, filling it clear to the opening. The entrance was then covered with smaller rocks so that it appeared much like any other part of the canyon.

Later that afternoon, as the women loaded possessions onto mules and the men readied the horses, the old chief called Polycarpio aside. He told him he was taking the tribe deep into Mexico and that now was a good time for him to return to his people. The following morning as the tribe rode and walked away to the south, the young Mexican stood alone at the spring, watching the Apaches until they disappeared over a far horizon. The year was 1877 and Polycarpio was eighteen years old.

Polycarpio told the chiropractor that he never felt any urge to reveal the secret location of the Apache gold until now, forty-nine years later. He told the doctor he would like to repay him for restoring his hearing by taking him to the Guadalupe Mountains and showing him the location of the old mine shaft.

Fascinated with the story related by the old Mexican, the chiropractor made arrangements to travel to West Texas with Polycarpio. Before the week was over, supplies had been purchased and preparations made for the journey, and within a few days the men departed by automobile for the Guadalupe Mountains.

Arriving at the tiny settlement of Pine Springs in the foothills of the range, the chiropractor left his car with a resident, borrowed two horses, and he and Polycarpio rode the short distance to the site of the old Mescalero campground near Manzanita Spring. It was evening when they arrived and the two men set up camp on the very site where the Mescalero Apaches erected their tepees and brush shelters decades earlier.

Following dinner cooked over a campfire, Polycarpio regaled the chiropractor with tales of living with the Apaches. Looking around at landmarks visible in the bright moon- and starlit-night, the old man recalled times of hunger, times of war, and times of joy. Presently, they crawled into their blankets and fell asleep.

The following morning after breakfast, Polycarpio led the chiropractor on a short hike to the nearby ravine that contained the gold mine of the Apaches. The walk was difficult for Polycarpio, and the rocky trail caused him to stumble and fall several times. Presently, they arrived at a point along the rim of the canyon where

Polycarpio paused and looked over the ravine below. Tiny pools of water were visible here and there, remnants of a brief rain only two days earlier. Birds flitted from tree to tree and the summer air was filled with the sounds of buzzing insects.

Suddenly Polycarpio stopped and excitedly pointed to a location on the floor of the ravine, claiming the gold mine would be found there. To the chiropractor, the place identified by Polycarpio looked much like any other part of the ravine.

After seating himself on the edge of the ravine, Polycarpio cautiously slid down the steep, rocky slope, the doctor following. At the bottom, Polycarpio led the chiropractor to a clutter of rocks near the opposite slope and told him the opening of the shaft was just beneath them. The two men labored for most of the morning moving aside hundreds of rocks. The work was difficult, and they stopped often to catch their breath. At one point, the chiropractor feared the old Mexican would surely succumb to heart failure, but Polycarpio bent to the task with a surprising enthusiasm.

By the time the sun was overhead, the chiropractor was beginning to despair of ever finding the gold mine. As he rested in the shade of a juniper, he was suddenly startled by a cry from the Mexican. Polycarpio was jumping about and pointing at something on the ground. Rushing over to him, the chiropractor immediately spied the outline of an opening to a shaft.

Excited at this validation of the existence of the old mine, the chiropractor worked with renewed vigor and without stopping for the next four hours until about five feet of the tunnel had been excavated. Exhausted, the doctor rested in the shade of a tree while pondering the monumental size of the task ahead of them. Following an extended break, he examined the shaft at great length and informed Polycarpio it would be impossible to lift out any more of the heavy rocks without the aid of some equipment and extra men. He told Polycarpio they must return to San Antonio and make arrangements to hire some workers and obtain pulleys and winches. Early the following morning, the two men returned the horses, retrieved the car, and left for San Antonio.

Back home, the chiropractor experienced considerable difficulty in locating the men and equipment necessary to remove the rock fill from the mine shaft. One delay led to another and several weeks elapsed. Then, on arriving at his office one morning, the chiropractor received word that Polycarpio Gonzalez had died in his sleep.

Because of the demands of his business, the chiropractor was unable to return to the Guadalupe Mountains until the summer of the following year. Arriving by himself, he examined the shaft once again and then proceeded on to El Paso where he tried in vain to hire men and lease some excavation equipment. Discouraged, he returned to San Antonio and his practice and finally gave up all hope of ever retrieving any of the Apache gold.

In the several decades that have elapsed since the chiropractor and Polycarpio dug into the old mine shaft, hundreds of thunderstorms have dropped rain onto the Guadalupe Mountains. The waters gather, converge, and rush down the slopes into the canyon and ravines toward the desert below. During these times, dense and heavy loads of fine gravel are transported by the short-lived yet swiftly flowing currents, debris that is often deposited along the way.

In this manner, the secret gold mine of the Apaches was once again covered over. Other flash floods may eventually remove some of the deposited material, exposing the opening to the shaft, but for the time being it lies hidden in the ravine that passes near the ancient campground of the Mescalero Apaches.

Chapter Eight

Pine Spring Canyon Treasure Chest

PINE SPRING CANYON is one of the best known and most completely explored canyons in the Guadalupe Mountains range. Extending for over three miles into a deeply eroded cut in the ages-old limestone, the canyon is embraced by Guadalupe Peak to the south and Hunter Peak to the north.

In 1858 the Pinery, a station for the Butterfield Overland Mail, was constructed at the mouth of the canyon. Several years later the tiny settlement of Pine Springs grew up across the road from the ruins of the Pinery. Both the station and the community were originally located there because of the availability of water and wood. These days, the springs are dry for most of the year, and the closest wood of any import grows at the higher altitudes.

During prehistoric times, Pine Spring Canyon served as home to early Native Americans. Evidence in the form of cave paintings and artifacts are often found in the canyon.

During the time of the Butterfield Overland Mail, the canyon was also used as a hideout by outlaws who found the protective walls, narrow passes, and abundant water and game to their liking.

During the first decade of the twentieth century, a man named Abijah Long arrived in the Guadalupe Mountains. A loner, Long spent much of his time prospecting in solitude deep within the range. After several unsuccessful months of searching for precious minerals, Long eventually contracted with Jim White to mine bat guano from the numerous caverns in the Guadalupes. White, the man who is often credited with discovering Carlsbad Caverns, had built up a successful guano mining operation and employed several dozen laborers.

A skilled and competent manager, Long was in large part responsible for White's company making an impressive profit in 1903. Unfortunately, the supply of and market for bat guano declined dramatically the following year and Long found himself out of work.

After leaving White's employ, Long moved to Pine Spring Canyon, living in his automobile while he constructed a crude rock cabin not far from the lower spring. For several years, Long earned a meager income hunting deer and elk and supplying game to area settlers. When not hunting, he roamed throughout the mountains, ever hopeful of discovering precious minerals.

While living in Pine Spring Canyon, Long became friends with Rolth Sublett, who visited the area often in search of his father's famous lost mine. According to area old-timers, Long had once known Old Ben Sublett himself and was convinced of the existence of his mysterious gold mine. On occasion, Long and the younger Sublett were seen exploring portions of the Guadalupe Mountains together in search of Old Ben's gold. When not searching for gold, Long would sometimes drive Rolth into Carlsbad for a weekend.

Long's closest neighbors were Walter and Bertha Glover who resided across the road in the tiny settlement of Pine Springs, raised cattle, and operated a small café. Long and the Glovers became good friends, and the sometime prospector was a frequent dinner guest at the Glover's household.

Eventually, Rolth Sublett grew too old and infirm to continue his quest for his father's lost mine. Long, on the other hand, continued to search the range for the legendary gold deposit at every opportunity. Once in a while he would invite Walter Glover to join him in the search, but the rancher always refused. Glover was never convinced gold could be found in the Guadalupe Mountains and expressed this conviction to Long many times.

One summer day in 1916, Glover noticed Long had been away from his cabin for two full days and nights. Concerned that his neighbor might have met with an accident, Glover decided to go look for him. While saddling a horse to go ride into the canyon, Glover spotted Long walking toward him along a winding game trail.

Long explained to Glover he had found some impressive mineral specimens near the head of Pine Spring Canyon and asked to borrow two horses to pack some of them out. Glover agreed to the loan of the horses, and Long told him he would stop by in the morning to pick them up.

Two days after borrowing Glover's horses, Long returned to his own cabin. As Glover fed chickens next to the coop beside his ranch house, he watched as Long unloaded several heavy canvas bags from one of the horses and placed them in the trunk of his automobile. An hour later, Long returned the horses and told Glover he was going to take the rock samples to El Paso in the morning and leave them for analysis.

Shortly after dawn of the following day, Walter and Bertha Glover were preparing for a day of ranch chores when they heard Long's automobile start up. Moments later, the car bounced down the rough canyon path and pulled onto the dirt road that led to El Paso. Long saw the Glovers and waved, and as Walter and Bertha returned the wave, the car was lost in a cloud of dust as it disappeared around a bend.

It was the last time Abijah Long was seen in the Guadalupe Mountains.

Fifteen years following the disappearance of Long, an investigator for the Wells Fargo Company arrived in Pine Springs asking questions about him. The agent was eventually directed to Long's old friend, Walter Glover, and during the next few hours of conversation between the two men, an amazing tale of lost treasure unfolded.

After driving away from Pine Spring Canyon, Long traveled to El Paso and arrived at the office of the American Smelting and Refining Company. Following an hour of negotiations with a company official, Long sold a large amount of gold in the form of nuggets. When the transaction was completed and Long was paid, he drove away.

Several years later and completely by accident, Wells Fargo officials came into possession of some of the paperwork relating to the sale of the gold and became suspicious. An elaborate investigation followed, and the story of Long's gold unfolded, a story that eventually brought the agent to the small, isolated community of Pine Springs, Texas.

During the conversation, rancher Glover related an incident that proved to be important to the case. Several weeks following Long's departure for El Paso, Glover was searching for some lost

Chest with "A Post" presented to JOHN N. CHAMBERLIN - by his friend, WALTER GLOVER.

FIG. 8 Treasure chest found in Pine Spring Canyon.
(AUTHOR COLLECTION).

cattle deep in Pine Spring Canyon when he made an interesting discovery. Riding near a shallow cave not far from Devil's Hall, a narrow pass in the upper reaches of the canyon, the rancher spotted a wooden chest. The chest, stoutly constructed of redwood and fitted with metal hinges and straps, was lying open and empty on the ground. Nearby was a broken lock.

On hearing the tale, the Wells Fargo representative asked Glover to take him to the chest, and after saddling a pair of horses the two men rode into the canyon.

According to the agent, the box to which Glover referred was a type commonly used by Wells Fargo to transport gold nuggets and dust via the Butterfield Overland Mail route. The agent surmised that this particular chest was one that had been reported stolen from the Pinery in 1859. Fully loaded with nuggets, the chest would have weighed just over four hundred pounds.

After the agent left, Glover retrieved the chest and displayed it in his café for several years. Eventually, he presented it as a gift to his long time friend, John R. Chamberlin.

Several months following the visit of the Wells Fargo representative, Glover learned that Abijah Long had been located in Oregon. Under questioning by law enforcement authorities, Long admitted to finding the chest in a cave in Pine Spring Canyon and selling the contents, the gold nuggets, for the sum of ninety thousand dollars. With his newfound wealth, Long traveled to Oregon, purchased a large ranch, and stocked it with prime cattle. Although Wells Fargo attempted to prosecute Long, it was determined by the courts that he had committed no crime in recovering and selling the contents of the chest that had lain undisturbed in a cave for approximately sixty years.

Some researchers contend that the gold retrieved by Old Ben Sublett may have come from this same Wells Fargo chest, and that the old man simply found the cache while prospecting in the mountains. Some have even speculated that Sublett may have been the one who stole the chest from the Pinery.

What is most intriguing is the fact that, according to the Wells Fargo agent who visited Walter Glover, not one but three chests containing gold were taken.

Were the other two missing chests hidden in Pine Spring

Canyon? It seems unlikely that only one would be cached and not the others. Were they ever found? If so, the discoveries have never been reported.

Many familiar with the details of Abijah Long's gold are convinced that the other two chests are still hidden somewhere in Pine Spring Canyon.

Chapter Nine

The Crow Spring Massacre

A SHORT DISTANCE across the desert floor beyond the western escarpment of the Guadalupe Mountains lies Crow Spring. This region, characterized by salt flats for many miles around, was a common stopping place along the trail to and from El Paso. Though the spring offered a rather brackish flow, it served not only travelers and explorers through this region, but Indian tribes as well.

As a result of the extraction of ground water in this part of West Texas for agriculture during the past half century, Crow Springs no longer flows with the vigor it once did, and for most of the year it remains bone-dry. Tall cottonwood trees, a rarity in this part of the Chihuahuan Desert, still mark the location of the old spring.

Crow Spring is on private property and can be reached only by obtaining permission from the landowner. Before the area was fenced off, the rare visitor to the spring forty or fifty years ago often encountered a variety of objects and artifacts partially hidden in the nearby desert sands. Arrowheads, metates, and scrapers provided evidence of generations of use by Apaches and earlier residents. The abundance of more contemporary artifacts is puzzling, however, for scattered among the dunes not far from Crow Spring are the remains of an entire wagon train.

Though most of the wagons and related artifacts have fallen victim to age, the desert winds, and decay, enough remain to suggest at least twenty wagons, all apparently carrying families and personal belongings, made a final desperate stand against attackers here. The remains of the wagons are arranged in a large, crude circle, suggesting the owners were either anticipating or preparing for an attack. The abundance of artifacts such as tools, books, pieces of furniture, pots, and weapons left behind, as well as human bones, leads one to believe the owners were all killed.

The remains of the wagon train near Crow Spring, along with snatches of tales told by locals and some obscure historical references, have led to the evolution over the years of the story of the Crow Spring Massacre. Based on what is known and what has been conjectured, the tale goes like this . . .

It was shortly after the close of the Civil War when the party of Germans left the small Pennsylvania settlement. Twenty wagons in all, many loaded just short of the point of collapse, pulled away from the town. From the wagons, women and children tearfully waved goodbye to family and friends, knowing they would likely never see them again. Bound for the newly opened lands in the Southwest, the wagon train wound along the trail until it was eventually out of sight of the townspeople.

Weeks of travel turned into months. Rains occasionally swelled rivers, making them impassable for days at a time. Flooded trails often caused wagons to bog down, requiring the efforts of several men and teams of oxen to free them.

The party of immigrants arrived in central Texas where they were enthusiastically greeted in the German-settled town of Fredericksburg. Here, the travelers rested themselves and their stock, replenished their supplies, and renewed old acquaintances.

The immigrants told their new friends they were seeking opportunities in the West. Many were farmers, some were trades-men, printers, carpenters, stonemasons, and furniture builders. They spoke of the fine homes they would construct, the fertile lands from which they intended to coax abundant crops, of churches and schools they would build. The residents of Fredericksburg could understand and appreciate these goals, for it was only thirty years earlier that they had done precisely the same thing on arriving from their European homeland.

When the day came for the travelers to depart, the Fredericks-burg citizens brought them food and drink for the first few days of the trip. Amid embraces, handshakes, and last-minute conversa-tions, the travelers arranged the wagon into a line pointed west-ward. Moments before departure, three men stepped forward and presented the leader with several boxes of cartridges. The dangers along the trail to the West were many, they explained, and they talked of the potential for encountering violent storms, drought, scarcity of firewood, and deep canyons. But nothing, they were told, offered more peril than the warring Indians they were certain to encounter along the way.

After listening to strong advice relative to maintaining a con-stant vigil against Comanches and Apaches, the members of the wagon train finally got underway.

More weeks of travel followed, but by now the party had

entered a different land, one entirely new to them, one characterized by aridity, few trees, and scarce water. Along the way, the
signs of the passage of Indians were abundant, but three weeks
had passed since leaving Fredericksburg and not a single one had
been seen.

At one point, the party encountered the remains of three wagons, all burnt and destroyed. Protruding from the sideboards of
the wagons were arrow shafts. Tied to one of the wagon wheels
was the shriveled corpse of what once was a man. Horribly mutilated, scalped, and set afire, the grotesque remains served to remind
the travelers of the earlier warning. After cutting down the body, the
Germans buried it nearby and conducted a small ceremony over the
grave. It was a somber group of migrants that continued westward.

Eventually the Germans arrived at Guadalupe Pass. Following
the long, dry, two-day climb up the gradually sloping foothills to the
cooler environment at the higher altitude, the travelers set up camp
next to the spring near the entrance of Pine Spring Canyon. Here
they remained for two days. While the women washed clothes and
made repairs to garments and wagon canvasses, the men refilled
the water casks and hunted game. Deer and elk were found aplenty
in the canyons, and mountain sheep could be seen leaping among
the rocks of the higher elevations.

The Germans were refreshed and invigorated by this new
environment, and as deer and game birds were cooked over
campfires that night amid singing and laughing, thoughts of hostile Indians and the burnt corpse encountered days before were far
from their minds.

After two days of relaxing in the camp, the leader of the wagon
train determined it was time to move on. The growing community of El Paso, Texas, was just over a hundred miles to the west,

and it was there they intended to stay for several days while they inquired about lands beyond.

By mid-morning, the ox-drawn wagons had labored down the steep trail toward the desert plains below. In the distance, the Germans could see the sunlight glinting off of what they initially believed was a huge lake. As they guided their wagons down the steep pass, however, they soon discerned it was only an extensive salt flat, as dry and barren as anything they had encountered along the trail thus far. According to the charts carried by the leader, the trail wound around to the northern end of the salt flat and there, he told the travelers, could be found another spring. By the time they reached it, they would have traveled about fifteen miles, a good day's journey in wagons. According to the chart, Crow Spring promised to be a suitable place to stop for the night.

By late afternoon, the cottonwoods surrounding Crow Spring could be seen in the distance by the approaching Germans. The leader rode ahead, deemed the area acceptable for an evening campsite, but found the water somewhat saline. As the first of the wagons arrived, he directed them toward a flat expanse of ground ideal for setting up camp a short distance from the spring.

As stock was unhitched and led to a nearby grassy area to graze, men and women busied themselves with camp chores. Several children roamed about the adjacent sandhills and played among the dunes. Just as the fires were started and preparations for dinner underway, the children came running in from the dunes shouting that they had spotted several horsemen to the north. Concerned, some of the men grabbed their rifles and went to investigate. Though they peered into the distance from the low ridges of the dunes, they could see nothing. Perhaps, they thought, the children just imagined they saw something.

Seated around the campfire that night, a number of the travelers thought they heard the neighing and whickering of horses several hundred yards to the north. Nervous and concerned, the leader doubled the guard around the camp and the livestock.

The night passed uneventfully, and dawn greeted the Germans clustered around the early breakfast fires. Following the meal, the animals were hitched up, wagons loaded, and the train readied for departure.

The sun was not long in the heavens when the first of the wagons pulled out onto the trail toward El Paso. Moments later, all twenty were moving single-file along the narrow route, enjoying the early morning warmth of the desert sun.

They had traveled no more than two hundred yards from the spring when suddenly the desert quiet was broken by a piercing scream and the thundering sound of oncoming horses. An Apache war party, forty to fifty strong, surged toward the slow-moving wagon train. As they neared, the stunned Germans saw the painted faces and menacing glares of the Indians. The Apaches, riding low upon the backs of their mounts, all carried bows, lances, and rifles.

Shouting in order to be heard above the din of the approaching warriors, the leader encouraged the drivers to arrange the wagons in a defensive circle. Few of the travelers heard him, but as the first wagons led the way, the others followed, and a somewhat disorganized loop took shape. By now, however, the Apaches were riding among the wagons. Arrows thudded into the bodies of men, women, and children. Some of the Indians leaped into the wagons, attacking and killing all within. Several of the young children were taken captive.

The massacre was over in minutes and the dead Germans lay upon the ground. While some of the Indians scalped the victims, others gathered up rifles, pots, pans, and tools. Three of the younger braves unhitched oxen and horses and pushed them together in a loose herd. Several other Indians broke open trunks and scattered the contents, taking what they wanted. When finished, they set the wagons and their contents afire. Two hours later, the Apaches, with the captive children and livestock and other booty, rode northward.

Behind the departing Indians, twenty wagons burned, the smoke drifting skyward until caught by an upper level wind and carried toward the mountains. Moments later, the first buzzard

FIG. 9 Sand dunes located west of the Guadalupe Mountains
not far from the site of the Crow Spring Massacre
(PHOTO COURTESY NATIONAL PARK SERVICE.)

appeared and after circling the burning wagon train for several minutes, was joined by others. Determining the ground below them held no threat, the circle of scavengers slowly descended toward the ground.

While much of this oft-told tale is conjectural, one can walk and dig among the ruined circle of wagon remains not far from Crow Spring today and find a great deal of supporting evidence for much of it—arrowheads embedded in wagon boards, human and animal bones, and personal belongings.

The actual identity of the travelers and their ultimate destination remain unknown. A search of historical records has shed no light on either, contributing to the mystery of the tale of the Crow Spring Massacre.

Chapter Ten

The Lost Tribe

LONG AFTER THE Mescalero Apaches were chased from their Guadalupe Mountains stronghold and placed on reservations in New Mexico, a few ranch hands and backpackers maintained that some few stragglers who escaped detection still remained in the range. It was alleged that these remnants of the defeated Mescaleros reportedly hunted game, harvested mescal, and found water in the many springs located in the area. Tales of Indians still living in the Guadalupes in a semi-wild state as late as the 1950s seem far-fetched, but occasional visitors to the range remained convinced it was so.

The largest force of Mescalero Apaches was driven from the Guadalupe Mountains during the bitterly cold winter of 1869. Led by Lieutenant Howard Bass Cushing, a group of sixty-five men, troopers as well as civilians, routed the Indians from their campground in a remote section in the range. Many Indians were killed, virtually all of their supplies, weapons, and shelters were burned, and a number of their ponies seized. Without stores or shelter, scattered rag-tag remnants of this once-proud and feared tribe lived a precarious existence in the mountains of West Texas and New Mexico until 1878 when most of them were finally rounded up and placed on the Mescalero Apache Indian Reservation near Cloudcroft, New Mexico.

Occasionally, a few Mescaleros at a time would escape from the reservation. Longing for the freedom of the mountains and days of glory derived from battles with the army, along with raids on area ranches, a few braves, and sometimes entire families, would ride away from the confines of the agency and flee to the Guadalupe Mountains. Here, they would live in relative peace until a detachment of soldiers eventually arrived and herded them back to the confines of the reservation.

The escaping of Indians from the reservation and into the Guadalupes continued off and on until 1912, according to the U.S. Government. In that year, they were once and for all rounded up and returned to the agency where authorities claimed they were permanently settled. When early Guadalupe Mountains settler Sam Hughes moved into and established a ranch in Dog Canyon in 1913, he often encountered abandoned Mescalero tepees and campsites. Hughes was told that they were left by the Indians who had been returned to the reservation the previous year, but some of the sites appeared to have been occupied since then. Concerned about trying to raise cattle in an area that might still be occupied by Indians, Hughes sought assurance from the federal government which, in turn, informed him that all renegade Indians had been cleared out of the range and settled onto the reservation some one hundred miles to the northwest.

But were they? Many have contended that not all of the

Mescaleros were removed from the Guadalupe Mountains and that they were occasionally spotted in the range for the next fifty years.

Though never documented, there have been dozens of claims of early cattle, sheep, and goat ranchers in this area that Indians were still living in the range. During the 1920s and 1930s, cowhands herding cattle in the high country meadows and searching for strays in the many remote canyons sometimes spoke of encountering fresh campsites and, rarely, small parties of Indians. Generally, the Indians appeared to be hunting on foot and, on spotting an approaching rider, would disperse into the forest. These mountain inhabitants were never hostile toward the cowboys. The occasional loss of a cow or calf was commonly attributed to the mysterious residents, but otherwise the growing herds of livestock were never threatened except by cougars and bear. It was also believed at the time that the Indians would come out of the mountains and occasionally raid some of the small gardens found near the few scattered residences.

During the 1940s, a Basque goat herder employed by the J. C. Hunter Ranch maintained a large herd of Angoras near Pine Spring. Here, the graze was adequate and the water plentiful. The Basque was a bachelor and preferred living alone in a small cabin that still stands near the spring. Many believe that the Basque is the only person known to have made friendly contact with the Mescaleros still living in the range. From time to time, the Indians would come down from the high country by way of the Bear Canyon Trail and fill their skins with the cool water that flowed from Pine Spring. At first, they would wait until the herder was off with his animals, but in time they grew accustomed to his presence and he to theirs.

During the 1950s, tales of Indians still living in the Guadalupe Mountains were sometimes heard in cafés and taverns from

FIG. 10 Remnants of the Mescalero Apache camp.
(PHOTO COURTESY NATIONAL PARK SERVICE.)

Cornudas to Carlsbad. Much of the talk was designed to frighten or impress tourists, and sometimes an old-timer would relate exaggerated tales about Indians raiding ranches and terrorizing travelers. It was, however, quietly accepted by many area residents that a few Indians were, in fact, still living in the Guadalupes.

Around this time, forest service employees occasionally stumbled onto game kills, butchered deer carcasses, and fresh campsites. Believing it was the work of area hunters, they thought little of it.

In the late 1950s, biologists and geologists conducting college and university field trips into the Guadalupes sometimes reported encountering recent campsites and campfires in isolated caves and under rock overhangs. In several instances, the remains of one or more elk or deer were found nearby. The occasional visitors to the interior of the range began to refer to the mysterious residents as The Lost Tribe.

During the early 1960s as more and more backpackers discovered the challenges of the Guadalupe Mountains, reports of Indian sightings grew more frequent. In one undocumented case, a backpacker related a story about being followed by an Indian for the three days he explored in the high country. The man, he said, was very dark-skinned, dressed in ragged, dirty clothes, had long black hair that hung below his shoulders, and sported a wide headband. He carried a handmade bow and arrows. The packer was convinced the man wanted only some food, and on his final day in the range he left behind two small bags of provisions.

After 1965, no one heard any more about The Lost Tribe. Some of those who kept up with the sightings over the years were convinced that, with the increasing numbers of hikers and backpackers in the region, the Indians simply abandoned the mountains.

Chapter Eleven

Juniper Spring Treasure Cave

IN 1930 A YOUNG goat herder named Jesse Duran accidentally discovered an incredible cache of treasure in a small cave somewhere along the southeast-facing slope of the Guadalupe Mountains. The find, a short distance from Juniper Spring, was to change Duran's life forever. It also generated a search for an amazing treasure that continues today, though its exact location remains a mystery.

In 1929, Duran, along with his family, migrated from Coahuila, Mexico, into Texas. While staying with relatives in Brackettville, Duran heard that J. C. Hunter, owner of the vast Hunter Ranch in the Guadalupes, was hiring cowhands and goat herders. In addition to grazing hundreds of head of cattle on the rich grass that grew in the foothills of the range, Hunter, responding to a growing demand for mohair, stocked a portion of his land with Angora goats.

Duran, though only eighteen years old, had spent most of his youth herding goats in his Mexican homeland. With his experience,

FIG. 11 Ranch foreman Noel Kincaid and J. C. Hunter.
(PHOTO COURTESY NATIONAL PARK SERVICE.)

he thought, he could surely obtain a job on the Hunter Ranch. After bidding his family good bye, the young man set out on foot toward the Guadalupe Mountains 320 miles to the northwest.

Duran arrived at the Hunter Ranch two weeks later and was immediately hired and placed in charge of a large herd of goats which grazed the eastern limits of the ranch. With a tow sack packed with tortillas, dried beans, coffee, and a small pot, Duran often remained with the herd for as long as two weeks at a time without seeing another human being. Springs in the area provided fresh, cool water, and once in a while a rider from ranch headquarters would bring him a fresh food supply.

Duran enjoyed working alone with the goats and took pride in watching them grow healthy coats of long, silky hair. While the herd grazed nearby, Duran took pleasure in relaxing in the shade of the trees that grew near Juniper Spring, his favorite water source in the area.

Duran was an uneducated and uncomplicated young man. Though he owned nothing of value, he cared little for material possessions, and most of the tiny salary he earned was sent to his relatives. The young man was a stranger to wealth, and as long as his basic needs for water, food, and shelter were satisfied, he longed for little else.

During February 1930 a cold, misty rain fell upon Duran as he watched the herd of goats grazing atop Rader Ridge, a low, narrow limestone spur that extends eastward from the southeast-facing slope of the Guadalupe Mountains. Jesse, wrapped in a warm woolen poncho, regarded his animals from the partial shelter of a Texas madrone tree. Noticing his canteen was empty, he decided to walk to Juniper Spring to refill it.

The spring was located approximately one mile southwest and

downhill from where Duran sat huddled against the bole of the tree. Taking one last look at the herd, he turned into the wind and struck out for the spring. After a few minutes of following the narrow goat trail that wound across the sloping foothills, Duran decided to attempt a shortcut across a section of limestone outcrop.

Duran believed the improvised route would shorten the distance to the spring and save time, but it proved to be somewhat tougher than the trail. The rain-slicked rock was slippery underfoot, and large slabs of broken limestone lay everywhere. Duran alternately walked around and on top of the slabs, occasionally knocking one loose and sending it skidding down the slope for a short distance.

When he jumped onto one large, flat slab, Duran felt it give way under him, spilling him to the ground. After picking himself up and wiping the mud from his clothes, the young herder noticed a small opening in the slope where the rock had previously rested. In the dim light of that cloudy morning, Duran stepped forward and peered into the small cave. As his eyes became accustomed to the dark interior, he recoiled in fright at what he saw.

Just inside the opening, propped up into seated positions against one wall, were three skeletons. Hanging loosely from the bones of each were the remnants of torn and rotted clothes. Leather boots, portions of which had been eaten away by rodents, covered the feet of two of the skeletons. Against the opposite wall of the cave leaned several rifles, at least six, Duran recalled in later years. On the dusty floor near the rifles, dozens of bullets lay scattered.

Then, Duran saw something that was to forever alter his existence. On the floor of the tiny cavern approximately fifteen feet from the entrance were three wooden chests similar to the type used by Wells Fargo and the Butterfield Overland Mail to transport valuables. The lid to one of the chests was open, and inside Duran could see hundreds of gold and silver coins.

Extremely frightened, the young goat herder could not bring himself to enter the cave. With considerable difficulty, he slid the heavy limestone slab back over the small opening, wedging it tightly in place. Still shaking from his experience, he continued on to Juniper Spring here he filled his canteen and returned to Rader Ridge where he pondered his discovery.

Later that afternoon after making certain the goats were secure, Duran decided to tell ranch foreman Frank Stogden about what he had found. He walked the several miles to Stogden's house, arriving about one hour after sundown. Mrs. Stogden greeted Duran at the back door and invited him in out of the cold and rain. After offering him coffee, she informed Duran that Stogden and three neighboring ranchers were playing cards in another room and would see him when they finished.

Approximately one hour later, Stogden called Duran into the room. While the foreman and his three friends listened in silence, Duran related his recent experience, carefully describing the skeletons, the rifles, and the three chests filled with gold and silver coins.

When Duran finished his story, Stogden and his guests began making plans to leave for the cave at first light and recover the treasure. Duran, however, was hesitant. He told the ranchers about his concerns, explaining that he greatly feared the spirits of the dead which he believed were guarding the cave and watching over all that was inside it. Duran explained that he was a devout Catholic and held strong beliefs in the power of departed souls. He also told them that he believed any treasure found in conjunction with skeletons was destined to remain where it was, and any who disturbed the site would bring hardship, perhaps even death, upon themselves and their families.

As Duran spoke to the men, his fear was evident, and the ranchers tried to calm him. They asked many questions, but the Mexican was reluctant to reveal much except that the cave was located approximately one-quarter mile northeast of Juniper Spring. Afraid they might frighten the young man away, Stogden invited Duran to sleep in the barn for the night, and in the morning they would continue their discussion about the treasure cave. The following morning, however, Jesse Duran was nowhere to be found and was never seen in the Guadalupe Mountains again.

Around 11:00 AM, Stogden and his friends arrived by horseback at Juniper Spring. After dismounting and hitching their horses to nearby trees, the four men began combing the area on foot. They searched the entire day but found nothing. On several occasions they encountered large, flat limestone slabs, but when shifted to one side no caves were found.

Stogden and his companions searched for Jesse Duran's treasure cave two or three times a week, chores permitting, for the next three months, but failing to find anything finally discouraged them to the point that they eventually abandoned the project altogether.

During the ensuing months, others learned of Duran's amazing discovery and soon the foothills of the Guadalupe Mountains were covered with treasure hunters. In spite of all efforts to locate the lost fortune, the mysterious cave remained hidden somewhere on the limestone slope.

The massive limestone reef that is the Guadalupe Mountains is pockmarked with hundreds of caves, some quite small, others such as Lechuguilla Cave and Carlsbad Caverns, impressively large. Within one mile of Juniper Spring, several small caves can be found.

Below the spring and about two miles to the southwest lie the remains of the Pinery, an important station for the Butterfield Overland Mail route that ran through Guadalupe Pass in 1859. At the Pinery, horses weary from pulling the coaches up the steep grade from the east were exchanged for fresh ones. Here, too, the passengers were fed. During its brief existence, the Butterfield Overland Mail was engaged in transporting money, supplies, and passengers from the east to the newly settled lands in the west. The line also carried shipments of gold and silver from the mining areas in the west to brokers, companies, and individuals in the east.

It is an established fact that desperadoes lurked in the remote environs of the Guadalupe Mountains, and it has been suggested that on occasion they held up coaches as the drivers carefully made their slow way up the steep grades toward the Pinery.

A few researchers have concluded that some of the loot taken during a stagecoach robbery was likely cached in the cave discovered by Duran. Some have suggested that the skeletons represent victims of the robbers, or maybe there was a falling out among the bandits themselves and three of the members were killed and placed in the cave.

Jesse Duran was known by several people in the Guadalupe Mountains area, and each insist that the young goat herder was honest, sincere, trustworthy, hardworking, and not inclined to make up stories about hidden treasure.

Several years after Duran's disappearance, it was learned that he fled to Carlsbad, New Mexico, where he remained hidden in the home of a sister for nearly three months, rarely going out-of-doors.

Duran's fear of the spirits was so strong that he continued to believe his discovery of the treasure was certain to bring bad luck to his own family. So terrified was he of such a thing that he decided to leave his sister's home and travel to California to find work in the agricultural fields there. In California, Jesse Duran lived and worked in relative peace until his death sometime in the early 1970s.

There is evidence to suggest that others may have found Duran's treasure cave. Sam Hughes, owner of a successful cattle and sheep ranch in Dog Canyon in the northern part of the range, was deer hunting one afternoon in the 1950s with several friends near Juniper Spring when he fell into a small cave. While walking along a bare limestone outcrop between the spring and Rader Ridge, Hughes accidentally slipped into the opening in the rock. Knowing that such caves often contained rattlesnakes, Hughes immediately scrambled out of it and continued on with the hunt. At the time, Hughes was unaware of Jesse Duran's discovery.

Later that evening as Hughes and the other hunters sat around a campfire and related the day's activities, the rancher told about falling into the cave. Noel Kincaid, foreman of the Hunter Ranch and familiar with the story of the lost treasure cache, asked Hughes to describe the cave and its location. To Kincaid's surprise, Hughes' description matched that given by Jesse Duran years earlier. The next morning, the deer hunters returned to the area but were unable to find it.

In 1966, a man named Lester White may have found the treasure cave but was unaware of what it was at the time. White, a graybearded, wind-blown, sun-wrinkled desert rat was a throwback to the days of the grizzled prospectors who lived for months at a time in the wilds as they searched for a gold strike or a hidden treasure.

Lured to the Guadalupe Mountains by tales of lost gold, White spent fifteen years in the mountains, only occasionally returning to his home in Artesia, New Mexico. Though White could relate many stories of hidden treasure in the range, he was not acquainted with the tale of Jesse Duran's discovery.

One evening White told a friend he had discovered a curious little cave in a rock outcrop about one mile northeast of the Frijole Ranch house, the former home of J. C. Hunter. White said he spotted the cave by accident one evening while he was resting alongside an old goat trail that led from Juniper Spring to the top of Rader Ridge. He claimed that just below where he sat next to the trail, the setting sun cast odd shadows from a large, flat limestone rock, shadows which suggested a deep hole. Approaching the rock, White noted that it had apparently slipped down the slope slightly sometime in the past, revealing a portion of the opening to a small cave. A small man, White was unable to move the heavy rock any further and contented himself with peering into the cave opening.

What Lester White saw caused the hair on the back of his neck to stiffen. Inside the cave, he said, were at least three skeletons, still clad in clothes and boots. In the darkness, White was unable to see into the cave beyond the skeletons, but he determined to return in a few days and investigate further.

White remained busy exploring and prospecting other areas in the Guadalupe Mountains and eventually forgot about the cave. Months later when a friend told White the story of Jesse Duran's treasure discovery, the old man recalled his earlier experience and decided to return to Juniper Spring. For several weeks, White searched throughout the area but was never able to relocate the cave.

In the exposed limestone strata between Rader Ridge and Juniper

Spring lie dozens, if not hundreds of flat slabs of rock of all sizes. In addition, here and there in the limestone can be found small holes, spaces eroded out between the layers of rock from countless ages of gradual groundwater movement. Slowly, yet with remarkable efficiency, this carbon dioxide-laden water dissolves the highly soluble limestone, eventually creating cave-like openings. In one of them lies three skeletons, a cache of rifles, and three chests filled with treasure.

Chapter Twelve

The Legend of John Seven Oaks

ONE EVENING DURING the late 1930s, a six-month-old baby was found behind the Pine Springs Café located near the top of Guadalupe Pass. The child, taken in and raised by Juan and Maria Seven Oaks, was called John by his foster parents. When John Seven Oaks was nine years old, Juan and Maria were brutally murdered by drunken cowboys from a nearby ranch. Though evidence gathered at the scene indicated young John may have been wounded or killed, his body was never found.

Some believe John Seven Oaks fled into the remote highlands of the Guadalupe Mountains he knew so well. Here, he lived for years in the wild alongside bear, mountain lion, and wolves. Some claimed to have seen him, others say he occasionally raided the gardens of foothills settlers for food. Some years later, the two men believed to be responsible for the killings of Juan and Maria Seven Oaks were found in a remote canyon in the mountains. Both men had been killed and beheaded, and the quiet talk in the area was that John Seven Oaks had finally gotten revenge.

As recently as 1977, bare human footprints were seen around the springs in the range, footprints many believe belonged to John Seven Oaks.

Moments after discovering the six-month-old baby in the dark outhouse behind the café, Bertha Glover summoned the county sheriff who, in turn, contacted law enforcement authorities in several states regarding a missing baby. After two weeks, the sheriff informed Bertha there was no report of such, and asked her if she would take care of it until arrangements could be made for its placement. Bertha agreed, but husband Walter cared little for having a baby in the house. A few days later, Bertha asked neighbors Juan and Maria Seven Oaks if they would keep the child until the sheriff could determine an appropriate course of action.

Juan and Maria Seven Oaks were Mescalero Apaches. Both in their forties, they lived in a small but well-constructed rock and frame house not far from Juniper Spring. Here, Juan herded goats, cut fence posts he sold to area ranchers, and hunted deer in the mountains while Maria tended a small garden. Childless, the Seven Oaks were at first overwhelmed by the responsibility of caring for the orphaned child, but they gradually settled into a comfortable and satisfying relationship with the baby. Eighteen months later, with the help of Bertha Glover and the sheriff, they formally adopted the child.

John Seven Oaks brought a fulfillment to Juan and Maria they had never known existed. The bright and happy child was a constant source of joy the couple never knew before, and each day was filled with love, sharing, and teaching. Juan took young John into the mountains on deer hunts and showed him the ways of the wild creatures found there. When the boy was very young, Juan carved a handsome little cross from a piece of cedar, strung a cord through a small hole he bored into the top, and presented it to his son. John cherished the cross, wore it constantly, and proudly showed it to visitors.

One morning when John was nine-years-old, a pair of riders approached the Seven Oaks' home while Juan was splitting firewood in the yard. Behind the well, John whittled a stick with a hunting knife given to him by his father. Drunk and barely able to remain in their saddles, one of the newcomers demanded liquor, and when Juan told him there was none on the premises, the rider drew a pistol and shot the Indian in the chest. Just before he fell to the ground, Juan hurled the axe with tremendous force, burying the head deep into his assailant's right thigh.

At the sound of the shot, Maria appeared at the open rear door of the house. Seeing her husband lying in the yard, she ran toward him, screaming. Just before she reached Juan, the second rider shot her down. After falling in the dirt with a mortal wound in her back, Maria Seven Oaks slowly, laboriously crawled across the stony ground and clutched her dead husband's hand. Seconds later she died.

Young John, on seeing his mother and father gunned down, ran from behind the well toward the two bodies, the knife still clutched in his hand. The sudden movement surprised the riders who, on seeing the gleaming blade, thought they were being attacked. Turning in the saddle, the first rider, the axe still embedded in his leg, raised his pistol and fired at the oncoming boy. The bullet struck John in the throat, and he fell, sliding on the gravel of the yard. He lay still, blood seeping from the horrible wound and spilling onto the ground.

After pulling the axe from his leg, the enraged killer dismounted and tied a bandanna around the wound. The other entered the house in search of whiskey. Finding none, the two men set fire to the structure, mounted, and rode away to the east.

Later that afternoon, John Seven Oaks regained consciousness. As he struggled to his hands and knees, he felt at the gaping wound in his throat, his shaking hand touching the torn flesh, coming away covered in blood and dirt.

The boy's attention was distracted by the smoldering embers of the house. Between him and the destroyed home lay his parents. Crawling to them, he lay beside the bodies. Tears poured from his eyes but no sound came forth. Because of his wound, no sound would ever again pass the lips of John Seven Oaks.

The next morning the sheriff, along with Bertha Glover and a handful of area ranchers, were poking around in the remains of the Seven Oaks home. It was puzzling to everyone present why anyone would harm this peaceful family and destroy their dwelling. What puzzled them even more was the fate of John Seven Oaks. Some advanced the notion that he was murdered or carried away by the killers, but the sheriff, after following a dim trail of blood for a short distance, was convinced the boy lived and fled into the mountains.

Juan and Maria Seven Oaks were buried near the burned-out home, their graves marked by slabs of limestone with their names chiseled onto the surface by Walter Glover. A four foot high chicken wire fence stretched tightly onto stout cedar posts was erected around the plot containing the two lonely graves.

The story of the brutal killings and the mysterious disappearance of John Seven Oaks was told and retold in coffee shops and taverns for months from El Paso to Carlsbad. Several theories were advanced but interest in the topic waned. Meanwhile, cowhands from the Hunter Ranch who rode into the Guadalupe Mountains from time to time to check on livestock would return with curious reports. A few claimed they had seen a youth deep in the dense woods, naked save for an animal skin covering his loins and wearing some kind of ornament around his neck. One of the cowhands attempted to pursue the youth, but lost sight of him after a few seconds. Bare footprints were sometimes seen in the soft earth, but since much of the mountain landscape consists of bare rock, tracking was impossible.

Over the years, residents in the foothills of the Guadalupe Mountains sometimes mentioned ripening vegetables mysteriously disappeared from their garden or fruits that had been taken from their trees. On rare occasions, houses had been entered and foodstuffs taken. In each case, sets of bare footprints were found in the yards, and John Seven Oaks was suspected.

Ten years after the killings of Juan and Maria Seven Oaks, the bodies of two area cowboys—Jake and Jesse Cruz—were found high in the Guadalupes. The sheriff initially suspected the Cruz brothers were involved in the Seven Oaks killings, but could never prove it. On the day following the murders, Jake was treated in a Carlsbad hospital for a deep wound in his right thigh, a wound that, according to the physician who treated him, was likely caused by an axe. The sheriff found a bloody axe in the yard of the Seven Oaks home. Cruz maintained he cut himself with a knife while skinning a deer.

Jake and Jesse Cruz had been sent by their ranch foreman into the mountains to round up stray cattle and herd them to the good grass found in a highland meadow called The Bowl. According to investigators, the brothers became separated. While riding along in a remote canyon, Jesse Cruz was busy looking for strays when he was suddenly pulled from his horse and knocked senseless. When he regained consciousness, he found himself tied to a tree with a cord fashioned from the fibers of mescal leaves. Facing him was a young man dressed in some kind of animal skin, but otherwise naked. In one hand the stranger gripped a knife and on his face was snarling hatred. A scar the size of a silver dollar covered the front of his throat.

Before he was able to say anything, Jesse Cruz was cut open from pelvis to sternum, his intestines spilling out onto the ground. Moments later, his head was severed from his body and wedged into the fork of a tree several feet away.

Two hours later, Jake Cruz, riding his sorrel along a dry stream bottom not far away, heard a sound in the brush off to his left. Since the foliage was too thick to allow for the passage of a horse, Jake dismounted, ground-hitched his animal, and walked into the cluster of low-growing brush in search of calves.

Moments later, while he was deep in the brush, Jake heard the sound of his horse galloping away down the canyon. Concerned the animal may have been spooked by a mountain lion, he turned and fought his way back through the dense vegetation. On reaching the place where he had left the horse, Jake was surprised to see a nearly naked man holding a drawn bow with an arrow nocked and pointed at his chest.

A split second later, the stone-tipped arrow thudded into Jake's chest, the impact knocking him to the ground. Still conscious, Jake squirmed violently and attempted to withdraw the shaft. A second later, another arrow smacked into his right shoulder. Then another, this one in the left thigh. Then another, and another, and within two minutes Jake Cruz, still alive, was screaming from the pain of nine arrows protruding from his body.

As Jake lay on the ground writhing in agony and wondering what sort of man this was before him, the archer dropped the bow, pulled a knife from his loin sash, and approached the dying man. The strange forest denizen grabbed the cowhand by the hair and pulled him to his feet. Eyes wide in horror, the last thing Jake Cruz felt was the sharp, cool sensation of the knife as it sliced his throat.

Four days later, the sheriff, in the company of a ten-man search party, found the bodies of Jake and Jesse Cruz. Though they searched the area where the arrow-riddled body of Jake was discovered, the head was never found. All around the murder scene, prints of bare human feet were found.

Though he never told anyone for years, the sheriff was convinced that Jake and Jesse Cruz were killed by John Seven Oaks as revenge for the murder of his parents ten years earlier.

Months later, a curious discovery caused Guadalupe Mountains foothills residents to wonder anew. Early one morning, Bertha Glover went to the Seven Oaks burial plot to place fresh desert flowers on the two graves. On approaching the small fenced plot, she spotted something out of the ordinary. Placed atop one of the fence posts was an object she couldn't immediately identify. On nearing the plot, however, Bertha reeled in horror on discovering a severed head, the dried skin pulled tightly across the skull, white bones gleaming under torn flesh. In the sand next to the post were the clear prints of human feet. Though never proven, the sheriff believed it to be the head of Jake Cruz.

Though a few suspected John Seven Oaks was somehow able to survive alone in the remote reaches of the Guadalupe Mountains, most were doubtful. The sheriff grew convinced that the boy had, in fact, lived in the range in a semi-savage state, but it was long after he retired before he was willing to admit this. To do so while he was a law enforcement officer, he said only weeks before he died in a Van Horn, Texas, nursing home, would likely have caused some embarrassment and invited ridicule from his fellow officers.

The closest thing to proof that John Seven Oaks survived for years in the Guadalupe Mountains came in the 1950s during a face-to-face encounter with a visitor to the upper reaches of the range.

Though forbidden to do so, the young niece of an area rancher went horseback riding into the high country. During this time, bear and mountain lion were plentiful, and it was whispered that Mescalero Apaches still resided in the remote canyons. By now, the tales of John Seven Oaks had achieved the status of folktale.

Unmindful of the admonitions from relatives, the girl, sixteen years of age, saddled a horse and rode the winding trail up Pine Spring Canyon and into The Bowl beyond. Riding along the pine needle-carpeted trail, the girl reveled in the majesty of the great Guadalupe Mountains forest and the powerful silence of this wild setting. Only the occasional screech of a pine jay broke the quiet of the warm morning.

Concealed in a patch of grass in the trail lay a coil of rusted barbed wire left over from a fence-building project of several years earlier. The horse stepped into the coil which became attached to its lower leg. Frightened, the animal bolted into the woods and along the edge of a deep arroyo. Knocked from the saddle by a low tree limb, the girl tumbled into the gully.

As she stood up and brushed the dirt from her riding clothes, she was startled by a sharp buzzing sound just behind her. Turning, she gazed in horror at a huge, coiled rattlesnake, its tongue flicking rapidly in and out as if tasting the air. A split second later, the snake struck, sinking its fangs into the girl's right calf. As the snake recoiled, the girl collapsed to her knees. Just as she believed she would faint, she was startled by the sudden blur of a figure that sped past her toward the reptile. Grabbing the snake just behind the head, the newcomer lifted it off the ground and, flashing a knife, severed it from the body in one quick motion. After tossing the writhing carcass several feet away, the stranger bent to examine the bite in the girl's leg as she lost consciousness.

An hour later, the girl awoke to find herself lying in the shade of a large tree not far from the arroyo. Her leg, badly swollen and quite painful, was wrapped in damp mosses. Standing nearby, she described later, was a nearly naked man of impressive physical appearance. Frightened that he might harm her, she feigned unconsciousness when the stranger examined her leg. As he concentrated on rewrapping a poultice of moss and spider webs, she noticed a hand-carved wooden cross hanging from a leather thong around his neck. Looking at the cross, she saw something that made her shudder—across the front of his throat was a ragged scar, evidence of an old and serious wound.

After the stranger finished tending to her snakebite, the girl tried to talk to him, but with hand signs he indicated he could not speak. Gesturing, he implored her to lie quietly in the shade of the tree. Taking one of her riding boots, he turned and strode away into the forest.

Hours later in the foothills below, a concerned aunt walked out onto the front porch of a ranch house. Wringing her hands in worry as she gazed up toward the high ridge of the Guadalupe Mountains, she wondered where her niece could be. Fearing for her safety, she moved to summon the ranch hands to undertake a search when she discovered one of her niece's boots on the porch steps. Picking it up, she heard the strange sound of something inside. Turning the boot over, the woman screamed as a sixteen-button rattle spilled out onto the wooden porch.

Within the hour, seven men on horseback, along with four tracking hounds, were riding up the steep canyon trail. The sheriff, summoned by the aunt, was at that moment driving up from Van Horn accompanied by a deputy.

Once at the top, the hounds had little trouble picking up the trail of the girl's horse, and within two hours she was discovered lying in the shade of a large spruce. As gently as possible, they transported her down the mountain and to the hospital at Carlsbad. The doctor who treated the girl explained to her aunt and uncle that whoever had provided the immediate though primitive treatment likely saved her life.

The next day, the sheriff, accompanied by the deputy, the girl's uncle, and one member of the original search party, returned to the location where she had been found. Examining the area for clues as to what took place, the sheriff discovered the remains of a seven-foot-long rattlesnake along with the severed head in a nearby arroyo. The rattle was missing.

Following the snakebite incident, reports of encounters with John Seven Oaks grew fewer and eventually ended altogether. During the 1960s, the few backpackers and hikers who entered the range returned with tales of spotting a man in the forest, a man who wore only a loin cloth, had his long hair held in place with a bandanna, and carried a bow and arrows. Forest service employees spoke of encountering human footprints near the fresh-water springs.

Since 1977 there have been no reported sightings of John Seven Oaks, nor have there been reports of footprints. When the federal government formally opened the Guadalupe Mountains National Park in 1971, hikers, backpackers, and trail riders entered and moved about the range in increasing numbers. A few familiar with the story of John Seven Oaks ventured the opinion that he may have grown intimidated by the growing numbers of people and simply went elsewhere.

Others who have followed the story suggest that by 1977, Seven Oaks would have been about forty years old and had lived in a primitive state for most of his life, a long time to survive in the wild. It is possible he could have succumbed to a rattlesnake bite, a fall, or some other type of accident. If so, his body has never been found.

There are those who believe that John Seven Oaks still lives in the mountains, surviving in the same manner he has for over sixty years at this writing. While it seems unlikely, it is not beyond the realm of possibility.

Chapter Thirteen

Headless Corpses

THE BEHEADINGS OF VICTIMS in the Guadalupe Mountains did not begin with John Seven Oaks. Stories that have circulated throughout the Trans-Pecos region since the 1880s suggested that the discovery of headless skeletons in the Guadalupes was not uncommon. In fact, if the stories are to be believed, as many as sixty headless skeletons have been found in or near the range since the 1930s.

As a young boy not yet in my teens, I often heard stories of headless corpses found in the Guadalupe Mountains, stories told by old-timers who had once worked as cowhands in the area, by men who were employed as firefighters and maintenance workers for the forest service, and by some who entered the range on a regular basis to hunt deer, elk, and bear.

Though the tales varied with the teller, they were all essentially the same—skeletons or shriveled corpses were encountered in the mountain range, generally in remote sections far from established trails. In each case, the skeleton or corpse appeared to have been beheaded, for no skull was ever found with the remains and there was evidence that the skulls had been severed from the spinal column.

On at least two occasions, according to stories, solitary skulls have been discovered, each of them far from any reported skeleton. In one case, the skull had apparently been placed on the green limb of a young tree long ago, for a small branch grew into the opening at the base and passed through one of the eye sockets. By the time it was discovered by a cowhand, it was impossible to remove the skull without cutting away part of the tree. The limb, with the skull still attached, was displayed for several years in a café in Carlsbad, New Mexico.

One particularly memorable experience involving headless skeletons was related by Simon McVay. McVay, an Ysleta, Texas, resident, was an employee of a gas company, and part of his responsibilities included visiting and evaluating pumping stations located throughout El Paso, Hudspeth, and Culberson Counties. During the course of his travels, McVay became closely acquainted with many of the area residents who in turn often invited him to accompany them on their hunts into the Guadalupe Mountains.

At the opening of deer season in 1947, McVay, along with three companions, rode horseback into the range. Ascending the old, steep, switchbacking route from Pine Spring Canyon to Pine Top Mountain, the riders led pack horses carrying tents, cooking gear, provisions, and rifles and ammunition.

Hours later after setting up camp in a clearing in The Bowl, one of the men walked into a nearby grove of trees to gather firewood. After a few minutes, he called out for his companions to join him, and when they did he pointed to a shocking discovery—a human skeleton, complete save for a missing skull. The man who discovered

FIG. 12 The Bowl.
(PHOTO COURTESY LAURIE WAGNER BUYER.)

the bones said they were under a pile of dead branches. When the hunters looked more closely, they discerned that an attempt had been made to hide the body, perhaps many years earlier.

After regarding the skeleton for several minutes, the four men decided to search around the immediate area for the missing skull. It was not found, but during the search, three more skeletons were discovered, each of them headless.

Fascinated with stories of headless skeletons, I began writing down accounts and searching for some myself. In 1955, when I was thirteen years old, I was invited to accompany a neighbor who wished to visit some relatives in Carlsbad. Knowing my interest in the Guadalupes, he promised to introduce me to some old-timers who had lived most of their lives in the area working for ranches.

The first of these early Guadalupe Mountains veterans I met were Walter Glover and his wife, Bertha, who owned the Pine Springs Café and operated a small ranch in the hardscrabble foothills of the range. After Glover and my neighbor exchanged pleasantries and discussed weather and livestock, I was invited to join in the conversation. Knowing nothing about interview technique at that young age I simply blurted out a question to Glover about the headless skeletons reportedly found in the mountains.

Glover, who I came to know better over the years, regarded me with a suspicious, even defensive, glare. After what seemed like a full two minutes of silence while his piercing eyes held my gaze, he leaned back into his rocker and asked me why I wanted to know. After I explained my interest and fascination, Glover leaned forward, tapped a tanned, weathered, and gnarly finger on my chest, and instructed me to find something else to get interested in, stating some things are best left alone.

I never learned why Glover felt compelled to offer that particular advice. Later that evening as my neighbor and I were returning to El Paso, I asked him about the old man's reaction. He told me Glover knew more about the subject than he would ever tell. I came away from the visit with Walter Glover more determined than ever to learn more about the headless skeletons.

In 1958 during a return visit to the Guadalupe Mountains, I met Ben Wattson. Wattson was a colorful character with a full mane of long, flowing, white hair and a beard that grew to his chest, who claimed to be over one hundred years old. Wattson and his wife Pauline were employed by the Glovers and lived in a refurbished chicken coop.

When Wattson wasn't busy with his chores, he spent most of his time exploring the Guadalupe Mountains in search of buried treasure. I asked him if, during his forays, he had ever encountered human skeletons.

Wattson pulled me aside, looked around to make certain Glover wasn't nearby, and spoke quietly. On two separate occasions, admitted Wattson, he had found human remains in the mountains. One was a skeleton, bleached white and in rather bad condition from exposure to the elements and having been gnawed on by rodents. The other, he said, looked more like a mummy, for it had dry, cracked skin stretched across the frame and was partially covered in what little was left of old, rotted clothes. The strangest thing about the remains, Wattson said, was that neither of them had skulls.

In the summer of 1977, I hiked several miles of Guadalupe Mountains high country one day with a National Park Service ranger named Lewis. One of Lewis' jobs was to maintain trails and pick up trash left by campers. Lewis relished this assignment, for it afforded him the opportunity to leave the trail now and then and explore some of the less visited areas of the range.

When I asked Lewis if he ever encountered anything unusual during his explorations, he admitted he had and said he would tell me about a very mysterious discovery if I promised not to say anything to his superiors. He did not want them to know he was doing anything other than what his assigned job called for.

About three months earlier, according to Lewis, he was checking on some hiking trails in the high country and found himself in a part of the range he had never before seen. After getting his bearings, he left the trail and explored an adjacent canyon for about two hours. On climbing out of the canyon, the ranger spotted what appeared to be a pile of tree limbs methodically stacked on a shelf of protruding limestone rock. Walking over to the shelf, Lewis pulled away some of the limbs and was startled to find a skeleton underneath. The skeleton was completely intact, he said, even down to the finger and toe bones, but the skull was missing. Lewis, who is no longer employed by the NPS, said it appeared as though the skeleton had lain on the ledge for a considerable time and it was somewhat weathered and rodent-chewed. An examination of the neck suggested to Lewis that the skull had been severed from the spinal column by a sharp instrument.

In all of the stories of the headless corpses found in the Guadalupe Mountains, none of the victims have ever been identified. In two cases, it was suspected that the remains were those of area cowboys who disappeared, but it was never verified. In another case, a skeleton was found that was believed to be that of a hiker who was reported missing, but no positive identification was ever made.

The absence of identity of any of the beheaded victims may be due to the suspicion that most of them were killed decades earlier when settlement in the area was sparse and the only people who entered the range were nameless hunters, prospectors, and Indians.

None of the discoveries suggest any of the skeletons belonged to recent victims. Bones, provided they are not eaten away by rodents, can last a long time in the dry semi-desert environment of the range, and it may be that many of them met their fate many decades ago.

Several explanations for the headless corpses and skeletons have been advanced. Many scoff at the notion that they even existed and insist the tales were made up to entertain or frighten tourists.

Maybe some were, but too many reputable men have told of their encounters with beheaded skeletons to dismiss the stories entirely.

Others have claimed the skeletons may represent victims of attacks by bear and mountain lions which live in the range. It has been suggested that, because some of the skeletons have been found partially buried or covered with brush, that animals were responsible. Mountain lions are known to cover their kills with brush and forest litter, returning later to dine on the remains. This explanation falls apart under close analysis. The black bear that live there will occasionally raid gardens and orchards, and both bear and lion have been linked to livestock losses. There are no records, however, of either threatening humans in the Guadalupes. Generally, these animals do not care to be around humans and simply move away when one enters their territory. Besides, predatory animals do not selectively remove skulls from their victims and carry them away.

A few have advanced the theory that the beheadings might have been the work of Apache Indians in the past. The Mescalero Apaches, who occupied the range for many years, were known to have returned in the early 1890s after escaping from the reservation, and were rumored to have lived there illegally as late as the 1960s.

None of these explanations hold up under careful examination, and today the headless skeletons of the Guadalupe Mountains continue to remain a mystery.

Chapter Fourteen

The Black Panther

DOES A BLACK panther live in the Guadalupe Mountains? Sightings of an ebony cat have filtered out of the range since the early 1940s, but solid evidence of its existence has been as elusive as the animal itself.

The first known sighting of a large black cat in the Guadalupe Mountains occurred during the 1940s when a Dog Canyon rancher observed one creep from its hiding place in a nearby arroyo and leap into the midst of some grazing sheep. After killing a lamb, the cat seized it in its mouth and bounded away, escaping up the steep slope of Manzanita Ridge.

Since that time, sightings of a large black cat in the Guadalupes, though not frequent, have occurred. Ranchers, forest service employees, hunters, hikers, and campers have reported encountering a black mountain lion in and near the range for over six decades.

A forest ranger once related a story that some time during the late 1950s he was followed for three days in the Guadalupe

FIG. 13 Mountain lion.
(PHOTO COURTESY NATIONAL PARK SERVICE.)

Mountains by a black mountain lion. The cat never threatened and appeared only to be curious.

Long-time Pine Springs resident Bertha Glover described an encounter with a black panther one night in 1960. As she was carrying garbage to a location behind her café to be burned, she said she saw a lion seated on a rock about twenty yards away. Glover said the cat was "blacker than the pit of Hades" but it made no move toward her during the few minutes she remained. The lion simply watched as Glover dumped the trash into an old oil drum and returned for more. When she returned, the lion was gone.

Glover saw a black panther on one other occasion in 1966. As she was sitting on a bench on the front porch of her café, she watched a black mountain lion chase a jackrabbit across the flat ground near the old Butterfield Overland Mail station about one hundred yards away.

In 1976, a backpacker came out of the Guadalupe Mountains high country with a black panther tale. During the entire time he was exploring the range, he said, he was followed at a distance of some twenty yards by a black mountain lion. When he stopped the lion stopped. When he continued, the lion fell in step, always maintaining the same distance. He said the black cat was lighter and thinner than a normal mountain lion, and the skull was shaped differently.

On his last night in the mountains, the backpacker watched from inside his tent as the black panther remained seated on the opposite side of a small, moonlit clearing. Eventually, the camper fell asleep, but was awakened a short time later by the sound of something at the front of his tent. He opened his eyes and saw the face of the panther pushing into the screen door flap as if to get a better view of what was within. The camper grabbed his camera and took a photograph, the flash frightening the animal away. He saw no more of it after that. The photograph, after it was developed, showed only a blur.

In 1990 a pair of backpackers returned from two days and nights in the range and excitedly described an encounter with a black panther. The cat, as in the other instances, merely sat quietly at a safe distance regarding the campers, making no attempt to approach. When one of the men walked toward it, the cat casually rose and strode several paces away.

The panther (*Felis concolor*) goes by many other different names in the Western Hemisphere—puma, painter, catamount, cougar, lion, and mountain lion. It is the only large, unspotted native North American cat with the exception of the jaguar, which is not uncommon in Mexico and South America, but rarely seen in the United States.

Once thriving throughout both continents, mountain lion populations are decreasing as human settlement increases. Hunting pressure and habitat destruction are the main reasons given for the big cat's demise.

When early Guadalupe Mountains ranchers began bringing large herds of sheep and goats into the area, their problems with the mountain lions started. The lions learned quickly that sheep and goats were easier prey than deer and elk and it was a simple matter to catch and kill them. Soon, according to the ranchers, the cats were reducing the herds at an alarming rate. One Dog Canyon rancher claimed he watched a large mountain lion run into the middle of a herd of sheep and indiscriminately slaughter twenty of them in a matter of minutes. It seemed, said the rancher, as though the lion was just having fun.

Consistent and enduring attacks on Guadalupe livestock

invited the hunting and trapping of mountain lions, and soon the population of these big cats in the Trans-Pecos region of Texas dwindled sharply. Though hundreds of mountain lions were killed between the 1920s and the present, not a single one of them was black.

Eventually, the mountain lion was placed on the federal government's endangered species list. Today, ranchers still report lion predation, and in spite of legislation continue to hunt them.

Despite reports of sightings, the black panther has never been authentically recorded in North America, according to the late lion hunter, researcher, and writer Jim Bob Tinsley. Each year, reports of black panther sightings from Florida to Arizona are filed, but one has yet to be killed, captured, or photographed.

The same is not true in Mexico, Central America, and South America. There, black mountain lions, as well as black jaguars, have been recorded, though they are uncommon. A rare large black cat, the onca, lives in Mexico. So elusive is this cat that only four or five photographs of it exist, and it was considered to be an imaginary animal until a hunter finally bagged one during the 1940s. It is remotely possible an onca migrated from Mexico into the Guadalupes, but more likely that a black-phase jaguar made the journey. Jaguars have been sighted along the Rio Grande in recent years some one hundred miles to the south of the Guadalupes.

It is possible, as some have suggested, that one or more black panthers migrated from Mexico and took up residence in the Guadalupe Mountains. It is also possible they are producing offspring. It is rare for a mountain lion to live more than twenty years in the wild, and since black panthers have been reported in the range since the 1940s, the consensus is that several must have resided in the area over the years.

While the neighboring sheep ranchers don't care to have large cats around, black or otherwise, others who have remained intrigued by the tales of the Guadalupe Mountains black panther like to believe that such a creature does indeed exist, and that it continues to fare well in the remote environs of the range.

Chapter Fifteen

Giant Snakes

It is believed by many that some American Indians can feel and see spirits that white men cannot. Anthropologists who study such things have written that the Indians place great importance on the spirits and take what they communicate very seriously.

A number of North American Indian tribes have legends pertaining to what have been referred to as the Snake People, a mysterious tribe, the members of which are believed to possess powerful medicine. Associated with these folk are dark powers of evil that few Indians care to talk about.

According to one legend, the Snake People were originally a tribe of Indians who lived in the Guadalupe Mountains long before the arrival of Spanish explorers. Here, they worshipped a giant rattlesnake that lived in a deep cavern. Occasionally, the Snake People offered one of their own as a sacrifice to the serpent. When other Indians migrated into the area, the Snake People would capture one now and then to offer to the serpent god.

FIG. 14 Diamondback rattlesnake.
(PHOTO COURTESY NATIONAL PARK SERVICE.)

In time, most of the Snake People left the Guadalupe Mountains and traveled to other parts of the continent. Carrying their secret and mysterious ceremonies with them, they often recruited members of other tribes to their ways, and researchers claim the rites long practiced by them have appeared in Navajo and Shoshone societies. According to the legend, the Snake People are able to breed with rattlesnakes and have the ability to transform themselves from humans to snakes in an instant.

It is whispered among some Indians that the giant rattlesnake still lives in the cavern in the Guadalupe Mountains along with a few members of the Snake People. To disturb the serpent god, according to the legend, is to invite a horrible death. According to the Mescalero Apaches, the best way to deal with these spirits is to avoid them altogether. It is said that when the Mescaleros lived in the range, they stayed far from the cavern that is the home of the giant rattlesnake, admonishing their young never to go near it.

During the 1940s, an elderly Mescalero worked for various sheep and goat ranches on and near the Guadalupe Mountains. His name has been lost to history, but his skills as a herder were so impressive that competing ranchers tried to lure him away. Sometimes, in a neighborly spirit, the Apache was loaned out to other ranchers to help with the livestock.

Once, while overseeing a large herd of goats on the southeastern slope of the range, the Apache stopped to have lunch with several Mexican herders in the shade of some trees near Juniper Spring. While the men were eating and enjoying their break, a large, thick-bodied rattlesnake slithered from under a nearby bush and into the view of the diners. The Apache, a look of horror on his countenance, jumped to his feet and warned the others that the serpent had been sent by the Snake People and that it was necessary to move to another location. The Mexicans laughed at the Indian, calling him foolish and cowardly. As the Apache shouldered his pack and prepared to move to another grove of trees, one of the Mexicans killed the reptile by dropping a heavy rock on it. Before leaving, the Indian warned the others that to kill a rattlesnake was to invite bad fortune.

The Apache's warning was to prove accurate. Within a week, two of the Mexican herders died from snakebites, and a third suffered a broken arm in a fall.

Several weeks later, the Apache decided to visit his sister who was married to a herder living in Dog Canyon on the north side of the range. Darkness had fallen by the time he reached the gate to their property, and as he moved to open it, the Indian was suddenly overcome with fear. In the air around him, he detected a strange odor that reminded him of angry vipers, and the sensation of evil was so strong and pervasive he felt as though he might collapse. Holding tightly to the gate, he opened it and entered.

The Apache looked around in the darkness as he closed the gate. Responding to a soft sound to his right, he turned and thought he saw a pair of large, slit eyes several yards away. Reflected in the glint of the eyes was a long, whip-like forked tongue, darting in and out of a great maw. The Apache wiped the sweat beading on his face, and when he looked up the frightening vision was gone.

While walking the half mile to his sister's house, the Mescalero was certain he had heard the sound of something heavy moving along the ground some distance away in the dark. Terrified, he continued on up the road. On reaching the house, he was greeted warmly by his sister and her husband, and that evening they dined on beef and beans and talked of old times and family.

During the conversation, the Apache's brother-in-law remarked at how difficult it was to earn a living these days and that he seemed to be losing more sheep and goats than ever to rattlesnakes. Sometimes, he said, the animals would just disappear, leaving no trace whatsoever. Occasionally some were found dead. A veterinarian who visited the ranch told the owner that one of the dead goats contained so much snake venom that its entire insides had dissolved.

At this point in the conversation, the Apache's sister broke down and confessed she had been offering sheep and goats to the serpent god to appease their anger and to keep them from killing members of her family. The ranch, she explained, was located close to the den of the giant snake, and the Snake People were demanding sacrifices.

As the two men listened intently, the woman spoke of the huge cavern that existed in the mountains nearby, a cavern in which, she said, lived the giant rattlesnake, the cavern to where the offerings were taken to appease the viper.

The sister said that, as a child, she was brought to the deep cave by her grandfather and warned about the evil serpent. The opening, she explained, is vertical and the pit itself is deep and dark. When she called down into the cave opening and threw rocks into the aperture, they heard the sound of what she described as "a thousand rattlesnakes."

Reports of secret ceremonies performed by the Snake People brought two government anthropologists into the Guadalupe Mountains during the 1940s to investigate. After locating the cave, the two men, despite warnings from area residents, decided to descend into it. After enlisting the aid of several nearby ranchers and cowhands, the scientists were lowered into it by ropes.

Once the men reached the bottom of the hundred-foot entrance, they went into the cavern. Within minutes, those at the top heard horrible, frightened screams, accompanied by a loud buzzing sound which reminded them of rattlesnakes. Frantically, they pulled up the ropes. One of the anthropologists was missing, the other, still harnessed onto the line, was dead. A subsequent examination of the corpse revealed that the body held an uncommonly high amount of rattlesnake venom.

Weeks later, a government bulldozer made its way to the location of the pit and proceeded to fill it with tons of rock, sealing it off. Two weeks later when inspectors came to examine the pit, many of the rocks had been pushed out of the hole and a new entrance was clearly visible.

Outside of a few Mescalero Apache Indians, few believe that the Snake People still reside in the Guadalupe Mountains. Reports of large snakes found in the region, however, have alarmed and fascinated residents and visitors alike for years.

At this writing, the official world record length for a diamondback rattlesnake is six feet, eleven and seven-eighths inches, yet snakes longer than that are found in and near the range with astonishing regularity. Professional herpetologists claim such a thing cannot be, but, as one rancher stated, the professors aren't around when the big snakes are found.

A book published in Europe in 1858 which chronicled the activities of a French missionary in Texas related an incident where a seventeen-foot-long rattler was killed. The reader was left with the impression that snakes that large were not uncommon in the American West a century and a half ago.

During the week that research for this story was being conducted in the Guadalupes, a large diamondback rattler was killed not far from the western slope of the range. The man who found it on his property near his house blew the head of the snake away with a shotgun at close range. Even without the head, the body measured just over seven feet long and was as big around as a grown man's thigh. The snake had thirty-four rattles, and a couple of old-timers said it wasn't nearly as big as some they'd seen in the past.

Few are aware of the Apache tales of the giant rattlesnake which legend claims still resides in the cave in the Guadalupes. Others who have heard the stories do not believe them and continue to venture unafraid into the region.

Once every few years, however, a hiker or backpacker fails to return from a few days in the high country. While the authorities ponder what might have happened to the visitor, the Apaches who live in the area whisper among themselves and claim they know. They say the Snake People have made another offering to the serpent god.

Chapter Sixteen

The Ghost Bomber

FOR YEARS, A MYSTERIOUS noise has been heard in the upper reaches of the Guadalupe Mountains. The sound, usually identified as an explosion, has mystified park and forest rangers as well as hikers and backpackers for decades, and explanations for its origin were slow in coming.

Today, it is generally accepted by those who frequent the hiking trails of the range that this strange noise has a ghostly origin.

Sometime during the mid-1970s, a group of backpackers who camped at the Pine Top campground reported hearing loud explosions. The sounds, sometimes as many as five or six during a single evening, seemed to come from one mile away to the northwest, somewhere near the eight-thousand-foot ridgeline. When the campers investigated, they found nothing. The explosions were described as powerful yet muffled, and echoes reverberated from the nearby canyons. Some of the campers even claimed that the ground trembled during the sound. When this experience was mentioned to National Park Service personnel, the rangers were mystified.

During the early 1980s as more and more backpackers and hikers discovered the fascinating interior of the Guadalupe Mountains, reports of the mysterious explosions increased. Now, however, those who heard them claimed they were often preceded by the sound of a large, low-flying aircraft. Though no plane was ever spotted, the sound was described as very loud. Once the explosion was heard, the sound of the aircraft ceased.

In 1985, a forty-eight-year-old backpacker who was staying at the Pine Top campground for three days and nights listened intently each evening as the explosions occurred over and over, each preceded by the roar of an aircraft. The camper, a retired air force navigator, recognized the sound of the airplane for what it was, a four-prop bomber, and the sound of the explosion, he said, was the impact of the plane crashing into the side of the mountain.

On the morning of the third day in camp, the backpacker hiked along the trail that winds across the edge of the escarpment from the campground to Bush Mountain some two-and-a-half miles away. He was searching for evidence of an airplane wreck, but found nothing.

In 1986, two backpackers, fresh from a three-day expedition in the Guadalupe Mountains, were taking breakfast in a Carlsbad café and discussing the odd explosion-like sounds they had heard at night. At an adjacent table, a local man who had heard their conversation introduced himself and asked if he could join them. He told the two men he had had an experience in the Guadalupes twenty years earlier that might have some bearing on the strange sounds.

During the 1960s, he said, he was working as a ranger for the

U.S. Forest Service and had been assigned to investigate some recent burns near Bush Mountain. As he was riding horseback along the trail to the site, he spotted a metallic object several yards away in the grass. Dismounting, he walked over to it, picked it up, and examined it. Unable to identify the item, he placed it in his saddlebag and continued with his work.

Two days later, the ranger showed the object to his supervisor who identified it as an essential piece of navigational equipment from the cockpit of a large airplane. Two weeks later, the ranger, along with two friends, returned to the location where the odd fragment was found. After tying their horses to a nearby tree, they walked into the low-growing brush that grew in dense clusters north of the trail in search of more fragments. After about fifteen minutes, one of the men called out and beckoned for the others to join him. Lying at his feet was a section of an instrument panel. The metal was bent and twisted, and the glass coverings of the gauges were shattered.

Within minutes, and only a few feet away, more metallic debris was found, and during the next half-hour, hundreds of pieces of metal fragments, oxygen tanks, and aircraft apparatus were discovered strewn across the hillside.

A short time later, the crushed and twisted fuselage and wings of a huge aircraft were found on the north side of the slope midway from the canyon floor to the ridge. Though clear proof of an airplane crash, this accident had apparently occurred decades earlier, for trees were growing through apertures in the wrecked plane.

Following the opening of the Guadalupe Mountains by the National Park Service in the 1970s, backpacking and hiking activities into the range increased. With more visitors reaching the upper elevations, the reports of ghostly explosions increased. Eventually, there unfolded an explanation for the origin of the mysterious sounds.

During the early 1940s, the United States was involved in World War II, and the government employed hundreds of airplanes in the effort, including fighters, transports, and bombers. One of the favored bombers was the B-24 Liberator. From a military base near El Paso, Texas, dozens of Liberators took off and landed each day as part of testing and training missions prior to overseas assignment. One evening, a Liberator, manned by a crew of five, was flying low over the plains of eastern New Mexico when it banked into a 180-degree turn for its trip back to El Paso. As the bomber proceeded westward toward the Guadalupe Mountains, it flew into a rapidly developing storm consisting of heavy rain and dense clouds.

Before the pilot could select an alternate course around the mountain range, the bomber was enveloped in the storm clouds and buffeted by the strong winds. Rain and hail pounded the aircraft while lightning illuminated the jagged crests of the Guadalupes for brief seconds. The plane was flying dangerously low and having difficulty gaining altitude. Finding himself in the heart of the violent storm, the pilot was faced with the problem of picking his way through the high mountain range with zero visibility.

The Liberator was doomed from the moment it entered the Guadalupe Mountains. Unable to determine direction or gain enough lift to clear the mountains, the B-24 slammed into the north side of a slope. All aboard were killed instantly.

Though the terrible accident occurred decades ago, the ghostly sound of the deadly crash, sometimes accompanied by the engine noise of the struggling Liberator as it tried to find its way out of the storm, is still heard today.

There is a bizarre addendum to this story.

Beginning in the mid-1940s, forest rangers and area cowhands working in the range reported encounters with what they believe was a ghost. From time to time, a man was seen in the vicinity of the Liberator crash site. The man, dressed in a military flight suit, was most often spotted walking through the low-growing brush on the north side of the trail. The image of the man is described as cloudy, as though he was enveloped in a mist. The figure appears to be confused as if he is lost or searching for something. When anyone calls out to or approaches the image, it disappears.

Since the mid-1970s, the strange apparition has been seen by at least a dozen backpackers. On one occasion, according to one of the eyewitnesses, the image called out for help.

The ghost, for that is surely what it is, may be that of a Liberator crewman who was left behind when the crash was investigated and the bodies recovered. Two days after the Liberator slammed into the mountainside, a group of five men, all dressed in military uniforms, arrived at the J. C. Hunter Ranch headquarters. After introducing themselves, they requested the use of horses to ride up to the crash site to investigate. They also requested a guide and extra mounts to transport the dead crewmen out of the mountains.

Noel Kincaid, foreman for the Hunter Ranch, agreed to guide the officers. During the ride up the trail to the ridge, Kincaid engaged a young lieutenant in conversation and learned that five men were aboard the aircraft when it crashed into the mountain. The officers, however, would discuss neither the mission nor any other aspect of the incident.

Riding along the trail from Pine Top to Bush Mountain, the party spotted a thin column of smoke rising from the still smoldering wreckage of the plane. After leaving the trail and guiding the horses down the north-facing slope of a canyon, they could see wreckage debris scattered across the terrain for hundreds of yards. Riding toward the smoke, the men discovered the remains of the plane. The Liberator had apparently slammed nose-first into the solid rock of the mountain.

Dismounting, the officers instructed Kincaid to remain with the horses and warned him against approaching the aircraft. With that, they went about their inspection of the wrecked Liberator.

Bored with his solitary assignment, Kincaid crept closer to the wreckage to obtain a better view. He was spotted, reprimanded, and escorted back to the horses.

About four hours later, four bodies were recovered from the wreckage, wrapped in canvas, and tied to the spare horses. During the ride back to ranch headquarters, Kincaid inquired about the fifth crewman, but the officers refused to answer his questions.

Several days later, Kincaid returned to the mountain to look around the plane for himself. In particular, he was curious about the fifth crewman, but he never found anything.

Today, many who hike and camp in the upper reaches of the Guadalupe Mountains are convinced the misty figure of the man in the green flight suit is the ghost of the missing crewman. Some have advanced the notion that he is searching for his companions. Others claim the ghost is simply dazed and wandering about trying to find some explanation for the disastrous crash.

Chapter Seventeen

The Ghost House

THROUGHOUT THE EXTENSIVE Guadalupe Mountains range can be found the remains of abandoned cabins. Some are near trails and visited by hikers, others are more remote and difficult to reach. Some have been forgotten over the years. At least two of the old cabins housed cowhands or sheep and goat herders stationed deep in the wilderness to watch over livestock. One of the cabins was constructed by some miners who lived in the area while exploring the possibilities of extracting copper from the mountains. Yet another was used by the U.S. Forest Service and served as a temporary residence for firefighters and as a storehouse for equipment.

Somewhere deep in the Guadalupe range may lie another dwelling, a house rather than a cabin. Over the years, a few hikers claimed to have seen it, and some have even claimed to have entered it, yet according to the National Park Service, no such structure exists. Park rangers who have gone in search of it have never been able to locate it. The mysterious and elusive dwelling, according to witnesses, may be haunted by a piano playing ghost.

During mid-May of 1974, a hiker entered an infrequently traveled part of the Guadalupe Mountains for a full day of exploration and photographing of the landscape. A veteran of numerous backpacking expeditions into these mountains, the young man was familiar enough with the environment that he often left the established trails to wander into remote canyons and parts of the forest seldom visited by man.

After setting up his tent at the Pine Top campsite, the hiker, carrying several cameras, a tripod, a daypack, and water, left the prescribed trail and found himself in a part of the range he had never seen before. The forest here was dense, and the thick canopy of trees kept the dim trail in shade most of the time. Ferns grew lush in the damp forest soil, and species of flowers found nowhere else in the world were blooming. Though this section of the forest seemed so dark and forbidding, the hiker noted that the trail he followed was a barely recognizable wagon road, one that had not been used for decades. Trees as big around as a man's thigh were growing between the ruts.

The diffused light that barely penetrated the thick tree canopy served to dapple the leaf- and pine needle-littered trail, providing for an eerie, wavering, shadowing texture. Oddly, no birds sang here, and the hiker stated later that the silence he experienced as he walked along was not unlike what he encountered while swimming underwater. He claimed he even felt a bit frightened, and gooseflesh rose on his arms from time to time.

Rounding a bend in the trail, the hiker spotted a long-abandoned house about forty yards ahead in an overgrown clearing. Unlike the log and plank and sheet metal cabins in the range he had visited before, this house was constructed of milled timber. The door was closed and the windows were all shut, and a dense growth of vines climbed the outside walls, struggling to meet at the apex of the peaked roof. The gray paint that once covered the structure was mostly faded.

As the hiker pondered the difficulties of transporting wagon-loads of lumber and other building materials into this remote section of the mountains, he pushed his way through the tall grasses and forest growth that encroached upon an old stone-paved path. Though he trod lightly, his footsteps seemed uncommonly loud against the stark silence of the surrounding woods. At one point he paused in mid-stride and looked around the old clearing, fearful he was disturbing the reigning peace of the setting. In the woods beyond, tiny unidentified creatures scurried through the grass and from tree to tree, and each sudden movement caused the hiker to jump.

The wooden porch creaked loudly when the hiker stepped upon it, the sound seeming to gain in volume as it traveled through the woods. Long unoiled hinges rebelled with a scream as he pushed open the front door. After casting a wary glance inside, he dropped his gear on the porch, took a deep breath, and stepped into the room.

Enough light filtered through the open door and the uncurtained windows to slightly illuminate the interior. From where he stood in what was once a living room, the hiker could see the kitchen and the entrance to a bedroom. The wooden floor of the living room was covered with debris and rodent droppings, and in the corners some of the wood was in advanced stages of rot.

More unseen creatures could be heard moving across the floor in the far room. The movement was not the hurried or panicked scurrying of animals fearing they will be seen, but rather a slow and deliberate kind, as if the little animals were waiting for the visitor to come into the room.

The interior walls of the house were covered with newspapers, pasted on several layers deep. The most recent date the hiker could find on any of them was 1917. As he read the faded print of some of the papers, he could hear the sounds of even more tiny animals moving about within the walls.

Against one wall of the living room stood an upright piano, the only piece of furniture in the house. In front of the piano was a wooden stool, apparently hand-crafted with great skill and fashioned from a deep-hued wood the hiker was unable to identify. As he regarded the piano, the hiker considered the effort it must have taken to transport this heavy, precious item along the rough roads and trails to this isolated part of the range. Whoever lived here must have appreciated music very much. The hiker also wondered why the piano was left behind when the residents abandoned the dwelling. Who were they? Why did they choose to live here. Why had they left?

Walking over to the piano, the hiker noted that it had only a slight covering of dust on the surface. It was days later when it struck him as odd that, while the floors and windowsills were thick with accumulated debris, the old piano and stool appeared as if they had been regularly cleaned, and used.

Tentatively, the hiker struck one of the piano keys and was mildly surprised when a clear, crisp note resounded throughout the room. He struck another key, then another. Then a few chords. Each of the ivory keys responded appropriately and, remarkably, the entire piano was in tune.

Pulling up the stool, the hiker began to play the instrument. Drawing upon an earlier time when he was more accomplished, he managed to get through an acceptable version of "Precious Memories," hitting only a few wrong notes. Encouraged, he went on to "Amazing Grace" and "Just a Closer Walk with Thee." Now lost in the joy of playing the fine piano, the hiker began to sing along as he fingered the keys. Each time he completed a tune, it seemed to him that the echo of the music resounded throughout the room for a full minute.

The hiker could not remember how long he remained in the old house playing the piano, but when he rose from the stool and walked outside, the sun had disappeared behind a western ridge, plunging the tree-encircled clearing into darkness. Fearful of becoming lost, he decided to undertake the long distance trek back to his camp. After gently closing the front door, he gathered up his belongings and made his way back along the overgrown wagon road to the main trail.

After breakfast the following morning, the hiker, carrying his camera and other gear, made the long hike from his campsite to Bush Mountain in the hope of photographing golden eagles. During one of his previous visits, he had spotted a pair of eagles soaring near the western escarpment, and since he learned their numbers were dwindling, he wished to capture their images in flight. After three hours of patient waiting, however, not a single eagle was seen, and the hiker was folding up his tripod when a ranger approached.

The ranger, who was inspecting the trails, was known to the hiker who had encountered him on previous visits, and the two men spent the next thirty minutes in pleasant conversation. Just before parting, the hiker asked the ranger about the old house he encountered the previous day.

The ranger paused a moment as if in thought and then asked the hiker to describe the house. As the hiker spoke of the wooden frame structure covered in vines and the piano in an otherwise empty living room, the ranger listened intently. When the hiker was finished, the ranger shifted his weight and looked out into the woods as he spoke.

The ranger told the hiker he had walked and ridden every inch of trail in these mountains during his many years of employment with the National Park Service and Forest Service. Years ago, when it was permitted, he often hunted in the range and claimed to know every canyon, cave, nook, and cranny. Looking back at the hiker, he told him there was no house such as the one he described in these mountains.

Just as the hiker started to speak, the ranger stopped him with a raised hand. He told him he wasn't the first person to mention the strange house. Though none who claimed to have seen the house knew one another, and though their experiences had been years apart, each described the house and piano exactly the same way.

Pausing for a second and regarding the ground upon which he stood, the ranger told the hiker something else. Some nights when he was camping in the high country, nights that were very still with little or no wind, the sound of piano music sometimes filtered through the trees from the direction of a rarely traveled portion of the forest. It was a soft sound, he said, strange and wavering. Sometimes it was clear, and sometimes only a hint of music could be heard. Though the ranger searched for years for the source of the music, he was never able to locate it.

During a subsequent trip to the Guadalupe Mountains, the hiker found his way to the deep forest where he had found the house months earlier. Though he searched for a full day, he was unable to find the house again, or even the wagon road that led to it. For several years following his first experience, the hiker undertook several systematic explorations into the range for the specific purpose of returning to the old house, but it always eluded him.

On two occasions, the hiker met other backpackers who claimed to have seen the house, and when asked described it exactly as the hiker remembered it. None of them, however, could remember where it was located.

In 1986, while camping near the Mescalero campsite along the Tejas trail, the hiker was awakened around midnight by what he was certain was piano music coming from far away. For nearly an hour he sat in his tent and listened to the barely audible refrains carried on the gentle winds.

Today, years later, he continues to search.

Chapter Eighteen

Mysterious Graves of Pine Spring Canyon

As LATE AS THE mid-1960s, only a handful of people knew the locations of the gravesites in the Guadalupe Mountains' Pine Spring Canyon.

Randomly distributed in seldom-visited parts of the canyon, the four gravesites were known only to cowhands, hunters, and a few hikers who frequented the area. The graves—low, elongated mounds of dirt sparsely covered with rocks and marked by thin, flat, rectangular slabs of limestone—were each treated with the customary reverence by all who passed them during their activities. Occasionally, when a headstone had fallen over, someone would prop it back up and dust it off. One of the gravesites even had a low wall of bleached limestone rocks stacked around it.

Names and dates of the deceased had been crudely scratched into the headstones, but decades of weathering had rendered them unreadable save for one where a name—Whatley—could be discerned.

During the spring of 1963 an amateur photographer from El Paso was camped for several days near Lower Pine Spring. Each morning following breakfast the photographer would hike into Pine Spring Canyon and spend the day photographing wildflowers, cacti, and interesting rock formations. The photographer had been visiting the Guadalupe Mountains and the Pine Spring Canyon area for several years and had become acquainted with a few of the herders and cowhands who worked for the J. C. Hunter Ranch.

During his explorations into Pine Spring Canyon over the years, the photographer sometimes passed near the gravesites. He occasionally wondered how the individuals interred within met their fates and why they happened to be buried in such remote locations far from any path. On this particular trip, the photographer was curious about whether they had been buried where they died or been killed, or if they were simply graves of men who lived in the canyon sometime in the past. Contented with taking photos of the lonely graves, the photographer moved on. On the afternoon of his third day in the canyon, the photographer loaded his camping and camera gear into his vehicle and returned to El Paso.

Several weeks later, the photographer arrived once again at Pine Spring Canyon and set up camp at his customary site. On his way home after two days of taking photographs, he stopped at a small café located on the highway near the Patterson Hills, a small range about five miles southwest of El Capitan Peak.

The proprietor of the café knew the photographer from previous visits, and the two men enjoyed conversing and relating tales and experiences pertaining to the Guadalupes. The photographer often brought pictures taken during previous trips to the canyon and showed them to his friend.

On this visit, the photographer spread about two dozen colc

images across the wooden table at which he sat, and together the two men looked them over. Picking up a recent picture of one of the gravesites, the photographer handed it to the owner and asked him if he knew anything about it. The owner said he had passed by this particular grave many times during hunting trips into the canyon, but could offer no information on who might have been buried there. During the next few minutes, the photographer showed him photos of the other three graves.

Presently, a man who had been drinking coffee at the counter rose, approached the table, and asked if he could see the photos of the gravesites. Thinking the stranger might have some knowledge of the graves, the photographer showed him the pictures. For several minutes, the stranger studied the photographs and then handed them back. Pulling a well-used topographic map from an inside coat pocket, he opened it up, laid it across the table, and asked the photographer if he could locate the sites of each of the graves for him.

For the next several minutes, the photographer pored over the map and, to the best of his recollection, marked the locations of each of the gravesites. After refolding the map and returning it to his coat pocket, the stranger thanked him, paid for his coffee, and walked out of the café.

During a subsequent conversation with the café owner, the photographer learned that the stranger came often to Pine Spring Canyon and sometimes camped in his car for days at a time. No one knew his name or what he did while there. He neither hunted game nor carried a camera. Now and then he was spotted by a herder or cowhand who would later comment that the stranger appeared to be searching for something.

Several weeks later, the photographer made another trip to the canyon. During the visit, his wanderings took him near one of the gravesites, so he decided to walk over to it. As he approached the grave, the photographer noticed a mound of dirt and cobble piled next to it. When he arrived at the site, he was shocked to discover it had been excavated. As he peered into the hole, he noticed the imprint within of what he initially believed was a casket. On closer inspection, however, he discovered the impression was much too small for a casket, being only a little over three feet long. Whatever had been buried in the grave had been removed.

Curious about the other graves, the photographer visited each of them and found the same thing—all had been dug up, and each bore the imprint of what appeared to be a narrow wooden crate.

Two days later, the photographer stopped again at the café on his way back to El Paso. When he walked in, the owner came out from behind the counter, led him to a nearby table, and invited him to sit down and listen to an amazing story.

The stranger who had been deeply interested in the locations of the gravesites stopped at the café three days after the photographer's last visit. When the owner asked him if he had any luck locating the gravesites that had been marked on his map, the stranger responded that he had not only found every one of them, but he had dug them up.

Stunned, the owner asked why. The stranger replied that he did so because they weren't graves at all, but caches of military rifles that were stolen from the U.S. army cavalry during the 1880s. The stranger then told the owner how he had learned about the story o the buried rifles from his grandfather, a man named Whatley, who along with a partner named Collins, stole the rifles during their shipment to some post in New Mexico. According to the grandfather, each of the cache sites was marked with a headstone intended to lead anyone to believe they were merely graves. Most people won't disturb a grave, the grandfather said.

Using the directions provided by the photographer, the stranger located each of the gravesites and dug up the crates of rifles. There were two crates buried in each grave, one stacked upon the other. Each of the crates held twelve rifles, all bearing the original grease with which they were coated at the factory. All were in pristine shape and had never been fired.

After spending hours digging up the crates and dragging them to a place where they could be loaded into his car, the stranger departed the canyon and stopped at the café to relate his experience.

When the owner expressed some doubt about the truth of the tale, the stranger went out to his vehicle and returned with one of the rifles, proudly displaying it to the doubter. Just before leaving, the stranger told the owner he already had a buyer for the rifles, a collector who had offered a handsome price for the lot. The stranger drove away toward the west and was never seen again.

As the photographer pondered this revelation, the owner leaned forward and said there was more to the story. According to the stranger's grandfather, the stolen rifles were buried in a total of six phony gravesites.

For the next several years, the photographer explored throughout Pine Spring Canyon in search of the two remaining graves but was never able to find them. To this day, as far as anyone knows, the two remaining caches have never been excavated. The likelihood is great that the headstones erected at each of the sites have long since fallen over, thus making discovery difficult.

In 1977, one of the remaining caches was discovered, although the finder was unaware the site was anything but a simple grave. A woman who had spent a day hiking deep in Pine Spring Canyon commented to friends that during her walk she had come across an old headstone that had apparently fallen over. Propping it up with rocks, she took a photograph of it, then continued on her hike.

One of her friends, a woman who was familiar with the story of the buried rifle caches, asked her if she remembered the location of the headstone in the canyon. The friend could not, but showed her the photograph she took. It bore an image of a slab of weathered limestone on which was crudely chiseled the name "Collins."

Chapter Nineteen

The Pinery Treasure Chest

ACCORDING TO A TALE told to only a few people during the 1950s, a wooden chest filled with gold was once buried at the Pinery, the station for the Butterfield Overland Mail located at the top of Guadalupe Pass.

One night, a stranger arrived in the area with a dog-eared diary, a portion of which described the gold and the location where it was hidden. The next day, the stranger and the treasure chest were gone.

From the 1800s to the present day, adventurers from around the country came to the Guadalupe Mountains to search for lost and buried treasure. Some possessed maps they were certain would guide them to the riches. A few employed metal detectors, and even fewer used dowsing rods to help them find the wealth they longed for. With rare exceptions, the treasure hunters came away empty-handed. In 1958, an event occurred that caused many to believe one of the lost treasures had been found.

For several years, an elderly gentleman named Ben Wattson

FIG. 15 Remains of Pinery, the Butterfield
Stage-Overland Mail station at Pine Springs, Texas.
(PHOTO COURTESY LAURIE WAGNER BUYER.)

was employed as a handyman by rancher and café owner Walter
Glover. Wattson's chores ranged from repairing chicken coops to
raking out the barn to cleaning up around the café and single-pump
service station. During lean years when the Glover's were unable
to keep Wattson on the payroll, the old man would find employment with area ranchers or other far-flung gas stations.

Wattson, affectionately called "Tio Ben" by those who knew
him, was a colorful character with a colorful past, and travelers or
Highway 62–180 over the pass never tired of listening to his tales o
adventure, banditry, and buried treasures.

Wattson was an unusual looking man for the 1950s. Tall, lean, and muscular despite his claimed one hundred-plus years, he sported a mane of shoulder-length white hair and a white beard that covered the top of his chest. He was never seen wearing anything but denim overalls. At the end of Wattson's left arm was a treacherous-looking hook instead of a hand. In spite of the metal fixture, Wattson could work and function as well as a man with two good hands. When he was in his seventies and eighties, he possessed an abundance of energy and was often seen hiking and climbing around in the foothills of the range.

According to Wattson's wife, Pauline, Tio Ben was born on a fishing boat near an island in Lake Michigan on October 6, 1863. Continuous and sometimes violent disagreement with his father caused Wattson to run away from home at ten years of age. For the next seven years, the youth traveled up and down the east coast working at odd jobs when he could find them and sleeping in alleys and forests. For a period of several months, young Wattson worked as a cabin boy on a ship that carried passengers across the Atlantic Ocean to France.

When he was seventeen, Wattson walked from New York to Texas, a journey that took several months. After arriving at the south panhandle settlement of Lamesa in 1880, he joined a group of westbound riders, and several days later they found themselves in the Guadalupe Mountains. Only after setting up camp deep in Pine Canyon did Wattson realize that his new-found companions were outlaws. The canyon was to be their hiding place from which they would range out in search of travelers, stagecoaches, and mail wagons to rob. The young Wattson was conscripted to work as a cook and take care of the horses. Virtually enslaved, he labored for the outlaws for three years without ever leaving the canyon.

On several occasions, Watson watched as three or four of the bandits would pack several days' worth of provisions into their saddlebags and ride out of the canyon. Days later, they would return, and packets of currency and sacks of gold would subsequently be divided among members of the gang. Wattson sometimes overheard accounts of depredations and killings, and during the time he remained at the outlaws' camp, he began to suspect that the roadsides from the mountains to El Paso contained numerous unmarked graves. At other times, Wattson watched as the outlaws cached chests and saddlebags filled with currency, gold, and silver in a number of different hiding places throughout the canyon.

One night when he was twenty years old, Wattson decided to escape from captivity. Crawling out of his bedroll around midnight, he crept over to the pole corral that contained the horses and made his way to a nearby canyon wall. For four hours, Wattson climbed the steep, rocky slope until he finally reached the ridge above. As dawn broke over Pine Canyon, it found him watching the outlaw camp from hiding as the men below discovered his absence. After searching for their cook for about thirty minutes, the outlaws finally gave up, packed their gear, and abandoned the canyon. On foot, and possessing nothing but the clothes on his back, Wattson crossed a portion of the Guadalupe Mountains and descended the western escarpment. After days of traversing the hot and dry desert to the west, he arrived in Silver City, New Mexico, where he found employment on a ranch.

For the next fifty years, Ben Wattson roamed throughout much of the western part of the United States. He found work on ranches as a laborer, farrier, breaker of horses, and general handyman. Sometimes he took jobs in town as a painter or handyman, and on two occasions he migrated to California and found work on ocean-going freighters which shipped goods to the Orient.

During the 1930s when he was seventy-two, Wattson married, and in 1939 he brought his wife to the Guadalupe Mountains where they lived for the rest of his life.

Ben Wattson was once asked by a writer why he never returned to the buried outlaw caches in Pine Canyon to dig them up. Though he possessed little in the way of money or personal possessions, Watson confessed to being very superstitious about buried treasure, a superstition he claimed he picked up from the Mexicans. Among that culture, he explained, it is believed a spirit guards lost and buried treasure. The spirit, called *El Patron*, would cause bad luck, even death, for the person who retrieved the treasure. In some cases, the bad fortune and hardship would even plague the relatives and descendants of anyone who dug up the treasure.

Though Wattson claimed to know where a number of buried treasures were hidden in the Guadalupes, he never touched any of them and revealed their locations only to his wife on the promise that she never attempt to search for them.

Ben Wattson died in 1963. Just a few months before passing, he provided the details of a buried treasure chest at the Pinery.

Ben Wattson was aware of the existence of the wooden chest filled with gold buried at the Pinery and had known about it for years. He once even located it using a dowsing rod, but refused to dig it up because he believed the rightful owner would someday show up to claim it.

From time to time treasure hunters would arrive in the range to search for fortune they believed to be buried near the Pinery.

Though the searchers often asked questions of Wattson, the old man remained silent or sent them off in other directions. One night during the summer of 1947 just past sundown, Wattson was sitting on a wooden bench on the front porch of the Pine Springs Café. He often retreated to this place following the day's chores and dinner. Here, he relaxed in the cool evening listening to the night sounds of the wild creatures that lived nearby.

Wattson was contemplating the arrangements of the stars in the clear night sky when he heard the sound of an automobile struggling up the steep road to the west. Presently, headlight beams pierced the night as the vehicle proceeded slowly along the rutted road toward the café. As Wattson watched in silence, the car, a black 1939 Ford which smoked badly, passed the building. After traveling another thirty yards, the brake lights came on and it slowed to a stop. Moments later, the driver turned the car around and pulled into the narrow gravel lot in front of the café. Opening a door that was in need of oiling, the driver climbed out, stretched, and called a friendly greeting to Wattson, who invited the newcomer to have a seat next to him on the bench.

When Wattson asked the man if he needed gas, he replied he didn't, that he required only some directions. Wattson stepped inside the café and poured a cup of coffee for himself and the visitor. After thanking Wattson for the coffee, the newcomer asked his host if he could provide some information on the location of the Pinery, the old station for the Butterfield Overland Mail.

In the glow of the stars accompanied by the small bit of light escaping from the café window, Wattson could see that the man seated next to him was a Mexican. He asked him why he wanted to know about the Pinery.

The Mexican explained that several years ago he discovered a diary in an old trunk. The trunk had been stored in the attic of a house in which his great-grandfather lived for many years. After the old man died, the family was going through the trunk when the discovery was made.

According to the diary, the great-grandfather had gone to California in 1850 during the great gold rush and, as a result of hard, back-breaking work over a period of many years, harvested an impressive amount of gold from a placer claim deep in the Sierra Nevada Mountains. When he was convinced he had panned all of the gold he would ever need to live on for the rest of his life, he decided to convert it into ingots and transport it to his home in San Antonio.

The gold was melted down and poured into crude molds he fashioned himself. He formed enough ingots to fill a wooden chest measuring eighteen by twenty-four inches. The great-grandfather, along with the chest, traveled from the mountains of northern California to Los Angeles. Here, passage was booked on a Butterfield stagecoach, and in the winter of 1859 he departed the coastal city for the long journey home. He intended to ride the coach as far as Fort Chadbourne, Texas, where he could disembark, purchase a wagon, and drive the rest of the way to San Antonio.

The trip from Los Angeles across the southwestern deserts was rough and tiring, and the stops at the remote stations along the way were a welcome relief to the jostling and bumping the passengers were forced to endure all day long. To pass the time during the long trip, the great-grandfather wrote in his diary.

On arriving at the Pinery station in Guadalupe Pass, the stagecoach driver was informed by the manager that bandits had been numerous along the trail ahead and that extra care should be taken.

For most of the night, the man fretted over this news and grew concerned about his fortune in the wooden chest. After some consideration, he decided to bury the chest in a secret location and return for it at another time when the threat of outlaws had vanished.

About two hours before dawn, the great-grandfather left his tiny room in the Pinery, crept out to the coach, and with great effort removed the wooden chest. As quietly as possible, he dragged the container into the station enclosure and then into his room in the north corner. During the next two hours, he excavated a three-foot-deep hole, placed the chest within, and refilled it. After his cot was returned to its normal position atop the cache, no one could tell that anything had been disturbed. The man intended to return to the Pinery with three of his nephews, retrieve the chest, and carry it to San Antonio.

As dawn broke over the pass, the station attendants were readying the horses for the next segment of the journey, the passengers were sitting down to breakfast, and the great-grandfather, sitting alone, was writing in his diary.

An hour later, the coach pulled away toward the next stop—Delaware Springs several miles to the east. Days later the great-grandfather finally arrived in San Antonio. Here, he told his family about the chest filled with gold and his plans to return for it. For the next three weeks, he made preparations to travel to the Pinery. His three nephews, well-armed and eager for the journey, joined him at his home.

Early on the morning of the departure as the team of horses was being hitched to the stout wagon they were to take on the trip, one of the animals kicked the great-grandfather in the head, killing him instantly.

Following the funeral, the nephews discussed the possibility of traveling to the Guadalupe Mountains to retrieve the chest of gold for themselves. Time passed, and the demands of their families and farms claimed their attention. Soon, the matter of the buried chest of gold was forgotten. Forgotten, that is, until the diary was discovered by the Mexican who sat next to Ben Wattson on this cool evening in the Guadalupe Mountains.

The Pinery about which the Mexican inquired was located across the road and just over one hundred yards away. Little was left of the old rock station and corral, for early settlers in this region scavenged many of the flat limestone blocks to build homes of their own. The outline of the Pinery was still evident, however, and at least two of the walls were still standing. It would be an easy matter to determine the location of the room in which the gold-filled chest was buried.

Wattson gave the Mexican directions to the Pinery. After another cup of coffee and more pleasant conversation, the newcomer thanked his host, climbed into his automobile, and drove down the road in the direction of the Pinery. Just before Wattson turned in for the night, he thought he heard the sound of a shovel being jammed repeatedly into the rocky soil.

The next morning after opening the café, Wattson decided to walk down to the Pinery to visit with the Mexican and see what progress he had made. As he neared the remains of the old rock structure, he saw no one was about.

Stepping into the enclosure, Wattson spied a mound of dirt near the north corner. Walking over to it, he noticed the hole on the other side of it. Peering into the excavation, Wattson saw the clear outline of a wooden chest at the bottom. The great-grandfather's diary had been accurate.

The chest must have been heavy, too heavy, in fact, to have been lifted out of the hole by one person. A slanted ramp had been dug so the Mexican could slide the chest up to ground level. From there, marks on the ground showed it was dragged out of the enclosure and somehow loaded into the trunk of his car.

Wattson never saw the Mexican again. Somehow, word of the discovery of the chest spread throughout the area, and once again treasure hunters by the dozen arrived to search for what they believed were more buried chests. With a mixture of amusement and scorn, Wattson watched the comings and goings of the treasure hunters and was visibly relieved when they departed.

Once, when asked for details about lost and buried treasure in the Guadalupe Mountains, Ben Wattson related that the mountains give up their secrets grudgingly, but only to those who have earned them.

Chapter Twenty

The Bear that Walks on Two Legs

FOR SEVERAL YEARS, a bear with an odd manner of locomotion lived in the Guadalupe Mountains. Though black bear are common in the range, this particular animal distinguished itself as a result of its unusual practice of walking on two legs.

In 1974, a Boy Scout troop from Dallas spent two nights at the Pine Top campsite. On the morning of the second day in camp, the scoutmaster led the youths on a hike into The Bowl, about two-and-a-half miles away via a rugged trail. Once at The Bowl, a number of the scouts, despite warnings from their leader, wandered off in different directions. About thirty minutes later, the scoutmaster gathered up his charges and noticed that he was three short. He was about to organize a search effort when he heard screams coming from the south. Seconds later, the missing scouts came into view, running as fast as they could toward the assembled group. When they rejoined their friends, the three breathlessly related an encounter with a bear, one they said walked only on its hind legs. The scoutmaster refused to believe the tale, but the three boys insisted it was true.

In 1977, a family of four was backpacking in the mountains when one of them had a similar experience. After a full morning of hiking along a trail that led to The Bowl, the family took a break in the shade of a large pine tree to eat lunch. While his father, mother, and younger brother stretched out on the ground and dozed in the warm sunlight, the ten-year-old proceeded some distance along the path, watching squirrels at play in the trees. Rounding a turn in the trail, the youth came face-to-face with a bear he described later as "hopping along on its back legs like a kangaroo." The boy turned and ran screaming back to his parents, but the bear did not pursue him. After relating his encounter with the bear, the boy's father insisted the youth was making up the tale. A while later the family continued with their hike, but the bear was not seen.

In 1980, a group of college students was exploring in and around The Bowl and collecting vegetation samples when they discovered bear tracks. Plainly visible in a section of bare soil recently muddied by rains were a number of prints. While the students made plaster casts of the tracks, one of the instructors noted something curious—only prints of the hind feet were visible.

A lone backpacker was hiking in The Bowl in 1984 when he encountered fresh bear scat. Continuing along a trail, he found several clear impressions of tracks along with more scat. On a stretch of trail, the tracks crossed an area of fine loam, leaving clear impressions. The hiker was startled when he realized that the bear that passed this way minutes earlier was apparently walking on its hind legs, for no front paw prints were visible.

Black bear are native to the Guadalupe Mountains, having existed here or centuries and surviving well on berries and rodents. When early settlers arrived in the area, the bear occasionally visited the lowlands to raid orchards and gardens and take an occasional calf or lamb or goat. After losing portions of their herds to bear, the ranchers set out to systematically hunt and trap the ursine predators. In the process, they killed hundreds.

Not only did the traps catch bears, they also ensnared bobcats, mountain lions, and coyotes, and after the passage of a few years, the predator population of the Guadalupes was significantly reduced. Though the number of black bears diminished, the two or three dozen that still resided in the range continued to make occasional raids on the lowland livestock herds.

Some animals fought the traps when caught. There are many cases on record of coyotes chewing off a foot in order to gain freedom from a trap. In at least one case, a bear is known to have left a foot in a trap.

Some time during the 1970s, a Dog Canyon rancher found the severed left front paw of a black bear while he was out checking his traps. The rancher followed the track of blood from the escaped bear for a half-mile until he determined it had retreated up into the range.

It has been hypothesized that the curious Guadalupe Mountains bear that walks on its hind legs may be the same one that lost a foot in the trap years earlier. The bear may have determined it was easier to get about walking and hopping on two hind legs than by limping on three or four. There is also the possibility that the bear may have lost its remaining forepaw in another trap, forcing it to move about on its hind legs.

Based on the available reports, the bear that walks on two legs has not been seen since the mid-1980s, and it is presumed the animal succumbed as a result of its reduced ability to hunt and forage.

Selected Bibliography

Allender, Michael and Alan Tenant. *The Guadalupe Mountains of Texas.* Austin: The University of Texas Press, 1984.

Anderson, Eugene. Interview, Pine Springs and Nickel Creek, Texas, 15 and 16 July 1985.

———. "Ben Subblett's Mine: Did it Ever Exist?" *True West*, September–October 1970.

———. "Hidden Gold of the Guadalupes." *True Treasure*, November–December 1972.

Armijo, Tony. Interview. Nickel Creek, Texas, 17 July 1990.

Bailey, L. R. (ed). *The A.B. Gray Report.* Los Angeles: Westernlore Press, 1963.

Ball, Eve. *In the Days of Victorio: Recollections of a Warm Springs Apache.* Tucson: The University of Arizona Press, 1970.

Bartlett, John Russell. *Personal Narrative of Explorations and Incidents of Texas, New Mexico, California, Sonora, and Chihuahua.* Vol. 1. Chicago: Rio Grande Press, 1965.

Bender, Averam B. "A Study of Mescalero Apache Indians." An unpublished manuscript prepared for the U.S. Department of Justice. 1960. Copy on file in Guadalupe Mountains National Park Library.

Biggers, Barbara. "An Ethnoprehistorical Study of the Mescalero Apache in the Guadalupe Mountains." 1979. An unpublished manuscript on file in Guadalupe Mountains National Park library.

Carroll, John M. (ed). *The Black Military Experience in the American West.* New York: Liveright, 1973.

Carson, Kit. "Lost Ben Sublett Mine." *True Treasure.* November–December 1968.

Conkling, Roscoe P. "Notes on the History of 'Pinery': The Butterfield Overland Mail Station on the Summit of Guadalupe Pass, Culberson County, Texas." No date. On file at the Guadalupe Mountains National Park library.

Conkling, Roscoe P. and Margaret B. Conkling. *The Butterfield Overland Mail.* Vols. 1, 3. Glendale, California: The Arthur H. Clarke Co., 1947.

Davy, Dava McGahee. *The Pinery Station*. Carlsbad, New Mexico: Carlsbad Caverns Natural History Association, 1979.

Dearen, Patrick. *Castle Gap and the Pecos Frontier*. Fort Worth: Texas Christian University Press, 1988.

Dobie, J. Frank. *Coronado's Children*. Austin: University of Texas Press, 1978.

———. *Legends of Texas*. Dallas: Southern Methodist University Press, 1924.

———. *Rattlesnakes*. Austin: University of Texas Press, 1965.

Dodge, Richard Irving. *The Hunting Grounds of the Great West*. London: Chatto and Wendies, 1877.

Glover, Bertha. Interviews. Pine Springs, Texas, 6 June 1961, 13 June 1965, 25 June 1971.

Glover, Walter. Interviews. Pine Springs, Texas, 6 June 1961, 13 June 1965.

Hughes, Woodie. Interview. Dog Canyon, Guadalupe Mountains National Park, 17 May 1980.

Jameson, W. C. *Buried Treasures of the American Southwest*. Little Rock, Arkansas: August House, Inc., 1989.

———. *Buried Treasures of Texas*. Little Rock, Arkansas: August House, Inc., 1991.

———. "Crazy Like a Fox: Lost Sublett Mine." *Treasure Cache*, 1993.

———. *The Guadalupe Mountains: Island in the Desert*. El Paso: Texas Western Press, 1994.

———. "The Juniper Spring Treasure." *Treasure*, March 1985.

———. "Lost Goatherder's Treasure, Part I." *Lost Treasure*, March 1991.

———. "Lost Goatherder's Treasure, Part II." *Lost Treasure*, April 1991.

———. "The Sad Saga of Rolth Sublett." *Frontier Times*, August 1985.

Jennings, Jim. "El Paso Gap. *The Cattleman*, May 1971.

Kincaid, Jack. Interviews. Nickel Creek, Texas, 16 December 1991.

Mulroy, Kevin. *Freedom on the Border*. Lubbock: Texas Tech University Press, 1993.

Timmons, W. H. *El Paso: A Borderlands History*. El Paso: Texas Western Press, 1990.

Tinsley, Jim Bob. *The Puma: Legendary Lion of the Americas*. El Paso: Texas Western Press, 1987.

Wattson, Ben. Interview. Pine Springs, Texas, June 1958, 13 August 1961.

Wattson, Mrs. Ben. *Hidden Gold of the Guadalupes*. El Paso: Tumbleweed Press, 1966.

Whitmer, Deana Kirk. Letters to author, 6 August 1985, 2 October 1985.

Worcester, Donald E. *The Apaches: Eagles of the Southwest*. Norman: The University of Oklahoma Press, 1979.

About the Author

W. C. Jameson is an award-winning author of fifty-five books, over fifteen hundred essays, and two hundred and fifty songs. He has recorded four CDs, written a musical, scored the music for two television documentaries and one drama, acted in five movies, and has served as an advisor for several television programs and one feature film. When not writing books, he travels the country performing his music at folk festivals, college campuses, and roadhouses. For relaxation, Jameson takes weeklong backpack trips into the Guadalupe Mountains.